MW01484060

HAND BOOK

Your Life is in Your Hands

Mark Seltman

Copyright © 2013 Mark Seltman

All rights reserved.

ISBN: 978-1497462618

DEDICATED

TO

EVERYONE

WHO

wants to understand their purpose

has a tough time being themselves

has a tough time making up their mind

has a tough time making up their heart

feels overly responsible, obligated, and guilty

questions everything or doesn't question anything

has too many acquaintances and not enough friends

fears dependency and intimacy

attracts strays and fixer-uppers

needs other people's approval

has too little or never enough

needs to be more spiritual

needs to be more creative

needs to be healthier

needs to be happier

TESTIMONIALS

Mark has worked with me personally as an interpreter of my and my family's hands and he has also joined events we hosted for clients at VOGUE Magazine. I recommend him 100%. He is expert in palmistry and tarot and he is sensitive to his customers so that he interprets what he sees in a thoughtful and insightful way. There is nothing "magic" about what Mark does -- it is truly all in your hands and in his ability to understand the individual he is helping. After so many years of working with Mark (over 10), he truly has become a trusted advisor and my admiration of him and his ability has only grown stronger. **Ann L.**

Thoughtful, inspired, and just, Mark is not only a consummate scholar of astrology, tarot and palmistry; he is intuitive in his scholarship. He meets you with an open mind and heart to deliver uncanny insights and doable suggestions for your growth. Life is an unfolding process and his art is all about nurturing your dreams with focus and hard work so that you can realize the auguries in the stars. **Randolyn Z.**

After mark did my reading, I spent a lot of time today thinking about his words. It was remarkably resonant, and inspired in me an incredible fascination with the depth and art of palmistry. Much of what he said I knew about myself, but there is something in the way he reads and speaks- with care, but also unafraid- that provides a certain kind of affirmation. It's as though these qualities I know about myself became truer, because now I am aware of constantly wearing them. I am completely in awe of the work he does. **Amalia W.**

I am a professional live event entertainment producer and Mark is the top of the top of readers based on client's responses. He is a reader clients continue to see privately-- guests feel transformed by his readings. **Tina B.**

Mark is easy going, great with clients and a wonderful entertainment option. I have hired him a number of times of corporate events and my clients from all over the world love him. Me too! Hire him and you won't regret it. **Tricia M.**

Mark has done readings for my company and clients for over 10 years now. In a word, he is AMAZING! He is intuitive, thought provoking and lots of fun. An absolute treasure to add to any party or event! I can't recommend him highly enough. **Michael Chaut**

CONTENTS
Acknowledgments

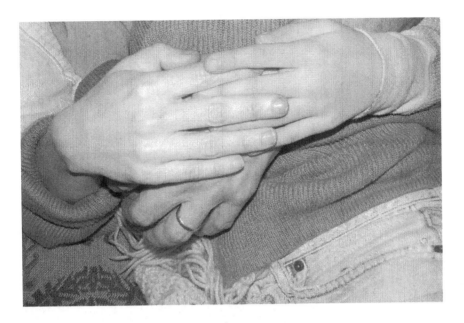

ACKNOWLEDGMENTS

I want to thank my palmistry teacher, Laurie Block Spigel, who inspired and encouraged me to take a leap of faith and do the work. I'm grateful to my wife, Joanna, who has been a supportive partner no matter what; my remarkable daughter, Cassie, who has taught me to be myself more than anyone else; to my wonderful parents, Cy & Micki, who always encouraged me to be me; to my in-laws, Joe & Sibyl, for loving us and supporting our choices; my brother and sister and their families who have always believed in me; a special tribute to Graham deWit, my nephew, who suddenly and unexpectedly passed away at age 23 in 2012. Graham would have loved helping me make palmistry viral. I also want to thank my extended and chosen families who I love and cherish from the bottom of my heart; and for everyone with hands everywhere.

INTRODUCTION TO REAL PALMISTRY

Before you read another word, look at your hands. What do you see, a confused jumble of lines and bumps? You're looking at a topographical map of your character in the past, present, and future. You can navigate your map and chart your course by knowing your hands.

Knowing your hands will guide you to become more conscious of your behavior, make healthier decisions, manage your time and free will better, and fulfill more of your innate talents and potentials. Your physical, mental, and emotional health is in plain sight at the ends of your arms.

You can ask your hands: Who am I? What do I value? What do I think? How do I feel? How can I best use my will power? How can I be healthier? How can I be happier? How can I understand my relationships better? How can I be more creative? What's my philosophy? What's my purpose? What are my hopes, wishes, and dreams? How can I be more spiritual? What's next?

Size, shape, and proportions of hands reveal a combination of four basic archetypes: Intuitive, Practical, Thinking, and Feeling. Few of us are pure types. We're a mixture of morphology and numerous qualities. Hand texture, color, elasticity, consistency of skin, and flexibility of joints reveal how well we initiate, maintain, and adapt to new ideas and circumstances. Lengths and proportions of fingers, knots, shapes of fingertips, and qualities of nails represent our relationships and how we are fulfilling our potentials in the world around us. Lines, dermatoglyphics (fixed skin ridge patterns), and gestures reveal more detailed information about our life choices and circumstances. The arts and crafts of interpretation and counseling require study and practice. I've created this book to show you that you don't have to be an expert palmist to gain insight from your hands. You need to know the basics, learn to be observant, and ask the right questions.

Astrology had been around for thousands of years when suddenly in 1968; Linda Goodman set the mass-market in motion with sun sign astrology. Horoscope columns suddenly appeared in newspapers and magazines. Linda Goodman's sold over 100,000,000 copies of her Sun Sign books with no e-social networking. Everyone began asking, **"What's your sun sign?"**

While serious astrology is based on an exact date, time, and place of birth and symbolizes a person's **potential** character, hands reveal **true** character; what we've done, are doing, and are likely to do with our challenges and potentials.

It's time for the ancient science and art of palmistry to be reborn, initiating exciting new opportunities for people to interact and get to know themselves and others better. A question for the 21st Century, **"May I see your hands?"**

Palmistry is simple and fun. My mission is to give people a helping hand, their own. I plan to affirm, confirm, and inform readers in constructive, helpful, hopeful ways. Compelling stories of clients, friends, family, and celebrities, and their hands will link ancient Greek mythology to present-day psychosocial narrative. As Joseph Campbell once said, "Oedipus crosses 42nd Street."

ABOUT PALMISTRY

"God has placed signs in the hands of all the sons of all men that all the sons of men may know his work"

OLD TESTAMENT

Palmistry is the 5500-year-old science and art of interpreting character from hands. Hands are topographical maps of human character in the past, present, and future.

The value of reading hands is in being able to readily recognize personality traits, motivations, habits, and patterns. As we identify strengths and weaknesses, we can change our thinking, exercise our free will, and transform our negative thought patterns into positive behavioral patterns.

We can take charge of our thinking, feelings, and actions while we examine our character, values, thinking, feelings, will power, health, relationships, creativity, philosophy, purpose, dreams, and spirituality. We can all be our own best friends and bullshit detectors.

The beauty of palmistry is: **hands change as thinking and circumstances change**. A tiny change in a line can reflect a huge change in a life. As we make decisions and exercise our free will, we get to see our successes and failures reflected in the mirrors of our hands over time.

Knowing your hands can transform your destiny.

Why is Palmistry so Obscure?

Most people think of palmistry as the dark and nebulous world of Gypsy fortune telling scams and curses. Sleazy storefronts adorned with large red neon hands flourish in cities with tourism. I've heard many reports of gypsy palmists who informed people that a nasty curse was preventing them from having significant relationships, satisfying work, or good health. The palmist will burn special candles and remove the curse for a hefty fee. People who are searching outside of themselves for answers to their problems marks them as potential prey.

Another reason palmistry is so obscure is that there's a sobering scarcity of good writing on the subject. Palmistry books are cookbooks: smorgasbords of unrelated details, inadequate ingredients, and unreliable recipes passed down for generations. Too many flawed colors, flavors, and textures ruin the meal. Palmistry texts are notoriously confusing, filled with inaccurate information, inferior illustrations, and cloaked in esoteric and technical jargon.

A majority of palmistry writers describe seven or eight basic archetypes while there are clearly twelve types. I've read hundreds of palmistry books and never a single word of dialogue between palmist and client. When an actual case history is mentioned, the palmist is usually 'talking at' a client instead of interacting with them. Too few palmistry writers emphasize the importance of free will. Exercising free will is the most important reason for learning to read hands.

The third reason palmistry is obscure is its location in bookstores: occult section, bottom shelf, nestled safely among the poorest selling, deadest inventory of astrology, numerology, tarot, and other occult divination books. While astrology symbolizes *potential* character and life challenges, hands reveal *true* character, what we've done and are doing with that character, how we're responding to our challenges and obstacles and fulfilling our talents and potentials.

The most important reason palmistry is irrelevant after 5500 years is that there's no spokesperson. That's my job. I hope to inspire readers to get to know themselves and others better. I plan to help seekers put their destiny exactly where it belongs, back in their own hands. The paradigm that palmistry is a world of gypsy fortuneteller scams and curses will finally be put into perspective and dispelled.

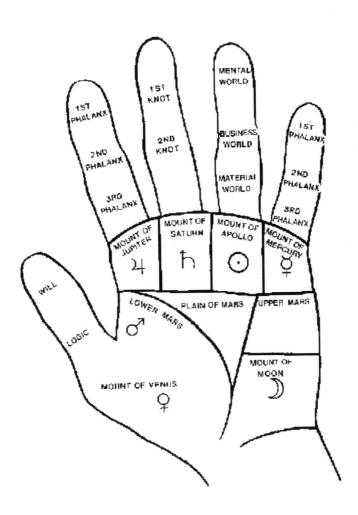

MY PALMISTRY EDUCATION

I'd never have pursued hand reading if I hadn't found a knowledgeable and powerful teacher, Laurie Block Spigel, who encouraged me to set aside my skepticism, take a leap of faith, and do the work. After studying the Benham system of western palmistry for three years and examining several thousand sets of hands, Laurie encouraged me to teach beginning palmistry students a series of ten rudimentary three-hour hand-reading lessons. I insisted on three key requirements.

1. If you can't be helpful or leave people feeling hopeful, don't say anything at all.
2. Practice what you preach.
3. Never predict anyone's death.

I encouraged students to look and listen carefully, think clearly and creatively, feel fully and freely, examine a multitude of hands, and ask abundant questions. Weekly reading assignments, study, and research were required. After completing ten classes, one student felt so confident in his abilities that he printed business cards and hung out his shingle as a professional palmist.

"There's no substitute for time and experience," I warned. "Proceed cautiously and lead with your heart," I advised.

A few months later, a very impressionable client showed up and told me about a palmist who had predicted her death. I asked to know the palmist's name. It was my ex-student. As soon as my client left, I called and confronted him. He denied the accusation. It's not uncommon for people to accuse readers of saying things they never said. It's happened to me. I didn't think that was the case with him. I promised to destroy his reputation if I ever heard another dark forecast. I haven't taught classes since, over 25 years.

I was a good judge of character, but that hadn't stopped me from making a wrong choice. I accepted a student's money, knowing he was dishonest, while rationalizing and idealizing how I would be "*the one*" to help raise his consciousness. I regret not asking him to leave when I saw how hastily he applied techniques he had learned in class to playing head games on people. Instead of kicking his butt to the curb, I scolded and cautioned him, then proceeded to give him more knowledge and tools to hurt people. It's easy to take advantage of others when you know what makes them tick. Prophecy is a powerful pill. People are impressionable. Only life predicts death.

WHY PALMISTRY?

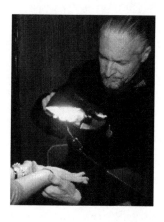

After a private consultation, people sometimes say, "I learned more in an hour with you than I did in six months with my psychiatrist". Of course, that's not true. Hand reading is prescriptive. It's no substitute for therapy. Recognizing or understanding something intellectually is only a first step toward working it out emotionally. An insightful and timely reflection can catalyze a change in a person's consciousness. At a corporate event last year, a man stood in line for over an hour for his five-minute reading to tell me that something I had said the year before had changed his life. I recognized a natural talent for writing and suggested that he take a writing class. Despite his being a huge procrastinator, he took my insight to heart, exercised his thinking and free will and took action. "What else should I work on?" he asked. He simply wanted me to affirm what he already knew.

Hands confirm and affirm what we already know. People give readers too much power. In fact, too many readers give themselves too much power. Recently, I saw someone on the street whose hands I'd examined for five-minutes at a corporate event last year. She proceeded to tell me how many of the things I said came true, even though I don't make predictions. She informed me of current events in her life as if I already knew they were happening. Meanwhile, I didn't even remember meeting her. I deleted her from my consciousness as soon as I finished reading her hands. On a busy week, I examine hundreds of hands. Every person is the most important person in the world for five minutes. My mind can get cluttered. Suppose I misinterpret some aspect of a client's character. That person might not challenge me because in their mind, my great reputation and specialized knowledge must make me right. We all need to learn to trust what we already know about ourselves.

Reading hands will not solve anyone's problems. Seeing something is one thing, working it out another. We cannot alter our past, but we can change our present and influence our future. No matter what our background, we still have free will to choose how we think and what we feel about what happens in our lives. As we focus our will power, we shape our character and corresponding destiny. It's time for hand reading to come out of the closet into the light of the 21st Century. Reading hands is a very potent form of self-help. Visualize examining someone's hands, looking into their eyes, asking them questions, and sharing their intimate thoughts and feelings.

HOW I BECAME A PALMIST

My family would have declared me mentally incompetent had I told them that I wanted to be a professional palmist forty years ago. We used to crack jokes about the middle class Jewish kids we knew from Pittsburgh who went to India or New York to study Metaphysics, find a Guru, or better yet, become a Guru. I was completely skeptical of symbolic languages like numerology, astrology, tarot, and palmistry, and utterly unaware of any hidden mysterious influences operating in my life.

There are more windows than beds

I was an ambitious product design graduate with a degree in industrial design from Carnegie Mellon University. The world was my canvas, my pallete overflowing with abundant natural resources and manufacturing processes. Endless consumers would be my patrons. I immediately hung out my shingle as a new product designer, manufacturer, and marketer. In only seven years, however, I managed to deplete an abundance of natural resources and pollute our environment in the name of fashion and ego.

My dad used to say, "Never say never." I thought he'd be around forever, instead, suddenly and unexpectedly, he died of a massive heart attack at age fifty-four. Dad was my Superman and Tarzan combined. He was my childhood hero, greatest fan, and best friend. I was my happiest self when I was with him. We frequently, dreamed of adventures we would have and good deeds we would do, just as soon as I earned that elusive pot of gold at the end of my rainbow.

Without dad to share my goals and achievements, my life disintegrated into a depressing routine of making things dirty, and getting them clean again and again. Troubled thoughts tossed, turned, and twisted in my head as I pondered god, fate, freewill, and destiny.

Maybe I wasn't supposed to be doing what I thought I was supposed to be doing.

So I meditated, got massaged, chiropractered, reikied, acupunctured, yogacized, analyzed, aerobicized, and aromatized. I explored Buddhism, Sufism, and Rosicrucianism. I attended classes in Astrology, Numerology, Palmistry, and Tarot cards with the best teachers in New York City. I showed up religiously at psychology, philosophy, and metaphysical lectures and workshops.

I joined the National Council for Geocosmic Research NCGR an astrological education and research organization. I was a member of the NYC faculty for over twenty years, speaking regularly at astrological conferences on the "horoscope in the hands". Inadvertently, I'd become one of those middle class Jews from Pittsburgh who my family and I had so thoughtlessly and carelessly judged and ridiculed.

I transformed from egomaniac to ecomaniac, becoming internationally known as the *Guru of Garbage* for my innovative uses of recycled materials and my *Designing with Garbage* classes at Parson's School of Design. Landfills were overflowing with award winning design. I was determined to make a difference. My greatest challenge was not having the proverbial '*pot to piss in*'. Clients used to say, "Why's it so expensive? It's only garbage." Even major Universities offered the most meager of stipends to speak with students about designing with recycled materials. I joined NYC's solid waste advisory board for two years and volunteered to speak to local community boards about recycling. Another seven years passed, however, I could no longer afford to save the world for free or preach to the converted for pennies. The chair below that I designed out of used milk and detergent bottles was a favorite of curators as it traveled across the country in a recycled seating tour.

Thrown

I readied myself to tackle the mother of all garbage, "*Psychic Garbage*". I convinced Cooper Union for the Advancement of Science and Art to offer *Metaphysics 101*. My three-hour lecture series presented an untraditional look at self and others through the lens of metaphysical symbolism. *Metaphysics 101* became one of Cooper's most popular public offerings. With fresh seekers showing up weekly, my class was moved to a large lecture hall. Everyone was looking for insight. I offered classes for five years and gave workshops and lectures at the New York Open Center, Learning Annex, East West Bookstore, Source of Life Center, Theosophical Society, Hunter College, Pace University, Marymount Manhattan College, Fashion Institute of Technology, Lower East Side Tenement Museum, and National Design Museum in Manhattan

I realized I had a gift for palmistry and began to build a clientele by reading hands at special events. Special event, meeting, and party planners retained me as a fortuneteller. I was a quickie character analyst, five-minute best friend and bullshit detector – great way to make a living and lots of fun.

When I began seriously reading hands over thirty-five years ago, my clients were mostly women. They signed up for my workshops and lectures and stood in line for five-minute readings at special events. Men showed up when their wives dragged them over. It was awkward holding hands with a man, looking in his eyes, and talking about his most intimate personal issues. Thankfully, that's no longer the case, although I'm sure being older and looking wiser helps.

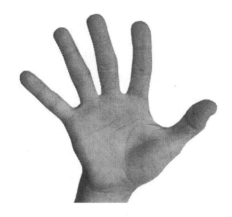

Your Palmistry Education

People ask, "How can I learn to read hands?" "Do you have a book?" "Why haven't you written a book?" I make excuses for procrastinating. Here are my favorite excuses: I hate generalizing. I love my anonymity. I refuse to be on the bottom corner shelf of the astrology section in bookstores. I won't waste trees. Does the world really need another Jewish self-help guru?

Although the science and art of palmistry is older than the pyramids, few people understand its true value. Reading character from the hands was first recorded in Vedic India about 3500 B.C. Chaldeans were interpreting character from hands in 1100 B.C. Palmistry spread to Greece and China. Aristotle wrote the first Western scientific treatise on reading character from the hands in 330 B.C.

Aristotle's work inspired Dr. William Benham, a skeptic who became the father of modern palmistry. Putnam Press published The Laws of Scientific Hand Reading in 1900. Considered the bible of western palmistry by most reputable hand readers, it's 650 pages long, dated, didactic in style, male chauvinistic in tone, and limited in scope. The Benham Book of Palmistry is its current incarnation. Rated the #1 palmistry book by palmists around the world, it ranks #13 on Amazon's best-selling palmistry books with a sales rank of 589,360. It's still worth reading, especially the first section on "Mounts of the hands". Modern palmistry writers continue to tweak and update unoriginal translations of Dr. Benham's work in unexciting ways.

The most famous palmist of all time was Cheiro. Born in Ireland as William John Warner in the mid-19th century, Cheiro called himself Count Louis Hamon, claiming noble ancestry that may or may not have been true. His stage name, Cheiro, comes from *chironomy* and *chiromancy*, the science and art of palmistry. Cheiro was clairvoyant, using palmistry, astrology, and Chaldean numerology to make surprisingly accurate predictions (mostly astrology and numerology), including major world events. Cheiro predicted the date of Queen Victoria's death, the year and month when King Edward VII would pass away, the grim destiny that awaited the Czar of Russia, the assassination of King

Humbert of Italy, and the attempt on the Shah's life in Paris. Mark Twain wrote this about Cheiro: "Cheiro has exposed my character to me with humiliating accuracy. I ought not to confess this accuracy, still I am moved to do so".

Many editions of Cheiro's books are still in print today in both English and foreign language editions and are available through Barnes and Noble and Amazon.com. They include his astrology book, <u>When Were You Born?</u>; <u>Palmistry, The Language of the Hand</u> (first self-published in 1897); <u>Cheiro's Book of Numbers</u>; <u>Cheiro's Book of World Predictions</u>; and <u>Cheiro's Palmistry for All</u> (rated #10 among palmists and #17 in Amazon's palmistry books - sales rank 1,681,713). My personal favorite, <u>Confessions: Memoirs of a Modern Seer</u> is out of print.

Cheiro was a sensational self-aggrandizing storyteller, which made his books especially fun to read. He always had plenty of juicy celebrity gossip to share, attracting many fans. Palmistry writings in his time were mainly didactic and fatalistic. Cheiro's content was exciting and fun, but imprecise. Many of his interpretations are blurred because he combined so many different metaphysical systems to make his assumptions and predictions. If Cheiro had been alive in this age of TV, radio, and web 2.0, he'd be a household name. His final years were spent in Hollywood, screenwriting and seeing over 20 clients a day until his death in 1936.

The Art of Hand Reading by Lori Reid (DK publishing) is a book I often recommend. Ranked # 4 by palmists - Amazon (Sales Rank 99,171), the 8 ½ X 11 hardcover version is a high quality beautifully illustrated book. It's well organized and in my opinion, the best of the cookbooks. Lori organizes information mostly by features in the hand. She devotes 26 pages at the end to "Applied Hand Analysis". While I don't agree with some of Lori's interpretations, I applaud her efforts.

Best-selling palmistry authors are not necessarily great counselors. A majority of authors are writers first, then palmists. Nat Altman has published six palmistry books including the *Palmistry Workbook*. He also writes about food, water, environment and other subjects. In my opinion, he's better than most palmistry writers, however, like most, I find his text dry and humorless. Richard Webster is another popular palmistry author. Three of his books rank in the top fifty among palmists. His books are mediocre at best in my opinion.

There are plenty of palmistry books out there. If you understand astrology, I recommend anything by Fred Gettings. His Palmistry Made Easy is ranked 959,475 on

Amazon and is available used for $.71, a worthwhile purchase. Judith Hipskind is another author worth reading. She has two books in the top 50 as rated by palmists. You can pick them up at Amazon for $.01 (plus shipping), an incredible bargain.

Hand Psychology by Andrew Fitzherbert is my favorite palmistry book. It's tightly organized and the authenticity of Andrew's interpretations makes it an interesting read. Rated # 5 by palmists, it's ranked 793,642 on Amazon's best-selling palmistry books list. I believe Andrew is one of a very few master palmists in the world. He approaches his clients and writing from a problem solving point of view. Many palmists are good at pointing out challenges, but they haven't a clue what to do with them. Some topics that Andrew has chosen to focus on are how to deal with difficult people, how to break a smoking habit, and how to solve employment problems. Andrew has just finished serving a very long incarceration in a penitentiary in Australia for committing a gruesome murder for which he was convicted. I wonder if he saw that in his hands.

Character

What is character? Free will forms character. Nature colors character. Nurture flavors character. Circumstance shapes character. Time tunes character. Character is destiny. Character can be seen in the hands.

People often portray character as if character were something good to have. If someone has character you can trust him or her. Character is not good or bad, but good and bad. Our character is the sum of our thoughts, feelings, ideologies, and experiences. Very few of us are pure types. We're the best and worst of twelve different archetypes whose relationships with each other form one huge dysfunctional family. Our collective and personal unconscious creates drama. Subconscious directs plot. Consciousness is stage-manager. As Joseph Campbell said, "Oedipus crosses 42nd Street".

Why do we have the hands we have? Why are we who we are? How much is nature and how much is nurture? My wife, Joanna, and I shared a unique opportunity to tackle the nature vs. nurture question first hand twenty- two years ago. I pulled our baby from Joanna's womb and cut her cord. Joanna tells the story of how I was reading Cassie's hands before I knew what sex she was. It's true. Her tiny hands could barely wrap around my index finger and they already had a tale to tell of her major life challenges that lie ahead; her strengths, weaknesses, skills, talents, goals, hopes, and dreams. Those tiny hands were beautiful, but on closer scrutiny, I felt confused and concerned. Cassie's index finger was very short. She'd have conflict with her self-esteem and spirituality. She also had a very short heart line, which I interpreted as serious, untrusting, and unable to articulate her feelings. Joanna and I have normal length index fingers and long expressive heart lines. We're very romantic and readily share our feelings. Why was Cassie so different from us?

Armed with knowledge and understanding, Joanna and I worked with Cassie to help her become as healthy, happy, and fulfilled as she could be. It took Cassie's formative years for her to learn to fully trust us. Had we been impatient, intolerant, or overcritical of her, she would have turned out very differently. Cassie worked hard to learn to think critically, to be decisive, and to exercise her free will in healthy ways. Luckily, she's naturally creative, philosophical, and spiritually aware. Her serious side is pragmatic, cautious, private, and brutally frank at times. She's a fabulous bullshit detector. Cassie's close friends appreciate her honesty. Her index finger and heart line have both grown longer and stronger over the years and continue to grow. She's gracefully unfolded with courage, strength, and dignity. Joanna and my index fingers have also grown stronger over the years.

Values

In the Jewish tradition when a child reaches the age of
thirteen he or she becomes a man or woman through a

religious rite of passage called a Bar or Bat Mitzvah. This ritual usually takes place in a synagogue and requires the terrified adolescent to read Hebrew from the Torah and sing in the religious service. There is usually a celebration afterwards in the afternoon or evening. I read hands at dozens of these celebrations each year ranging from modest family gatherings to multi-million dollar extravaganzas. I work with the world's best magicians, caricaturists, and entertainers at these events. I'm the *Psychic* (it's entertainment) with my lighted magnifying glass. Over half a century after my own Bar Mitzvah, kids call me Gandalf, Dumbledore, and Merlin (works for me).

Adolescents queue up for their five-minute hand reading. I try my best to pinpoint their strengths, weaknesses, and pressing issues. Some kids don't take what I do seriously, frivolously asking, "What's my boyfriend's name?" or "Am I going to win the game or pass the test?" It gets a bit tiring after several hours. When they're too demanding, I have to remind them that I'm not one of their servants. Parents make a huge fuss over their Bar Mitzvah kid on this special day. Numerous large flat screen TVs play perfect family moments for all the guests to see. Mom and dad give brilliant speeches about how incredible their child is and how proud they are of him or her. Then at some point during the party the kid comes to see me. Some are healthy and happy, while others are emotional basket cases (disasters waiting to happen), and many of their parents don't have a clue. A lot of wealthy kids have everything but what they need the most (and it's not stuff). What we see on those huge screens is often a distorted snapshot of the truth. Sometimes, I ask kids to bring their parents over so that I can chat with them about what I'm seeing. You'd think a party is an inappropriate setting for discrete counseling, but most parents usually appreciate my being frank with them.

I used to say to my palmistry students, "It's not what you see, but you say and how you say it that matters". It's amazing how many kids ask, "Will I be rich and famous?" In response to a *Thinking type*, I may ask, "Will satisfaction and fulfillment in your relationships and career be enough for you?" I may say to a *Feeling type*, "You'll look back one day and realize that your greatest riches resulted from being vulnerable and intimate with your family and friends." I might tell an *Intuitive type*, "If you don't feel inspired or passionate about whatever you choose, all the wealth and fame in the world won't matter." If the question comes from a *Practical type*, I'll ask, "What's your plan?" In my charitable work, I sometimes examine the hands of sick, impoverished, or homeless kids. They rarely ask about fame. Instead, I hear, "Am I going to be OK?"

One evening, I watched as an entourage' of kids escorted their friend to his hand reading. He looked like a little businessman in his very expensive designer suit and tie. He was a *Practical type* with small soft square palms and short pudgy fingers. It was obvious that he'd never done a lick of physical labor. One of his friends enthusiastically addressed me, "Do you know **who** he is?" To me, he was one more pampered kid with various talents, abilities, and challenges. Turned out, he was a son of one of the wealthiest families in the world. I asked his hovering fans to quietly back off while I spoke to him about working harder to express his true feelings and about learning to behave more naturally. I could see from his eyes and body language that I wasn't getting through. It was more important to put on a good show for his friends than listen to me.

At the end of the evening, he came back by himself and sat down as if we had never met. I tried to reach out again, offering the same advice as before. As soon as I finished, he exclaimed, "I fooled you. You already read my hands." "I know who you are" I answered, "You're the little (last name) boy and I'm going to offer you some very valuable free advice". I looked directly into his eyes while firmly holding his hands. "Your money doesn't make you better than anybody else. Your power is unearned. You'll grow up and be old one day, just like everyone else. You'll have relationship, work,

40

and health challenges and problems. What's important is for you to decide what you truly value. How do you plan to use your abundant resources to make positive differences around you?" He slinked away with rounded shoulders. I hope I made a meaningful impression

Values are relative. Everything has value. Everything and nothing are identical in nature, but different by degree. The billionaire dying of cancer would gladly trade his wealth for youth and good health. The famous opera diva whose child is brain damaged, would gratefully scrub toilets in Grand Central Station if it would bring her child back to good health. What and how much do we have to lose before we learn to value what we already have or have taken for granted? It's in our hands...

Will Power (part 1)

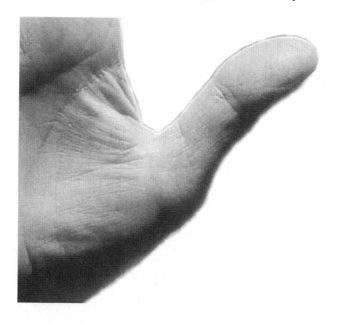

Our hands manifest the messages of our minds. In turn, our characters, thoughts, feelings, and experiences are mapped in the shapes, proportions and topography of our hands. Because hands change as thinking and circumstances change, we can make decisions and exercise our will power, then observe those changes in our hands over time. Exercising free will is the most important reason for learning to read hands.

The thumb is the site of will power in our hands; it's the reason we have dominion over our simian ancestors. The thumb is a small body part that takes up huge space in the cerebral cortex of our brains. Our minds develop because our thumbs oppose our other four fingers. All tools, from a simple pencil to our most complex computers are a result of the placement of our thumbs.

Thumbs symbolize our most valuable human resources: will power, logic, and ability to love. These three priceless qualities must be balanced in order to live a healthy, happy, and fulfilling life. Like the other four fingers, a thumb has two joints that create three separate segments known as phalanges. The first or top phalanx of the thumb represents will power. The second or middle segment represents logic and reasoning ability. If the will phalanx is longer than the logic phalanx, a person acts before he thinks. If logic is longer, he's good at figuring things out, but gets stuck in his mind. He procrastinates on making decisions and taking action, although a bit more logic than will power keeps him in check. The third or bottom segment is the ball of the thumb, which is contained by the lifeline. The ball of the thumb determines our capacity for love and our ability to maintain intimate relationships. It also indicates our ability to empathize, nurture, and appreciate other people, as well as animals, nature, art, food, and music. Logic and will are misguided without love and empathy.

Thumb size is very important and needs to be judged in relationship to the hand as a whole. Is your thumb large or small in comparison to your hand? The top of an 'average' length thumb is level with the middle of the bottom phalange of the index finger. Shorter than this indicates a short thumb, longer indicates a long thumb. A long thumbed person is a natural leader who wants useful and practical results. Unless the will phalanx is especially long, thinking is the guide. A short thumbed person is guided by his heart and easily led by first impressions and sentimentality. A very short thumbed person may have trouble being motivated enough to get out of bed in the morning. He can get addicted to watching television or playing solitaire on his computer while he avoids responsibility. I encourage these people to join a gym and to impose schedules, structure, and discipline on themselves in order to build their will power and take pride in something they've accomplished. The only way to build will power is to exercise it.

Thumb size is very important and needs to be judged in relationship to the hand as a whole. Is your thumb large or small in comparison to your hand? The top of an 'average' length thumb is level with the middle of the bottom phalange of the index finger. Shorter than this indicates a short thumb, longer indicates a long thumb. A long thumbed person is a natural leader who wants useful and practical results. Unless the will phalanx is especially long, thinking is the guide. A short thumbed person is guided by his heart and easily led by first impressions and sentimentality. A very short thumbed person may have trouble being motivated enough to get out of bed in the morning. He can get addicted to watching television or playing solitaire on his computer while he avoids responsibility. I encourage these people to join a gym and to impose schedules, structure, and discipline on themselves in order to build their will power and take pride in something they've accomplished. The only way to build will power is to exercise it.

Will Power (part 2)

Story Time: Three Little Pigs and their Thumbs

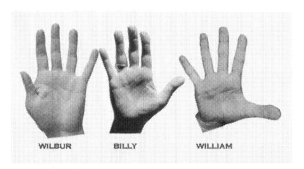

Once there were three little pigs that were brothers. Wilbur had tiny thumbs, Billy had medium size thumbs, and William had large thumbs.

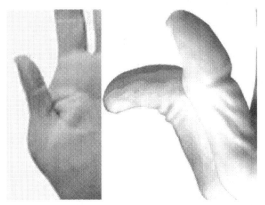

Wilbur's high-set tiny thumbs were very supple. The top phalange flexed back easily at the first joint. He was sweet and kind, a real romantic, but with those conical tips, lived in a world of his own ideal fantasies. Wilbur dreamed of having a beautiful home, riches, and true love, but he didn't understand the importance of making commitments, having determination, or being loyal. He didn't have a clue how to make his dreams come true. He played lotto, hoping to solve all of his problems at once. When a fellow pig was down on his luck, Wilbur would give him what little resources he had, then run to his larger thumbed brothers and ask for a handout. He'd offer his latest poem or sing them a song, hoping to engage their sympathy. Sometimes Billy and William would get so frustrated that they'd deny Wilbur's requests. He'd brood and tell strangers of the unfairness of his brothers and of the world in general. Putting it mildly, this little pig was unmotivated and unassertive and the world is not particularly kind to little pigs with these qualities. In school, Wilbur enjoyed art and music, but performed poorly in academics. It's not that he wasn't smart, but he didn't apply himself to anything. Other pigs of questionable character easily led Wilbur around. He was constantly falling in love, building elaborate romantic fantasies in his imagination, but he was so shy that the object of his desire never even knew he existed. If only Wilbur's parents had known about thumbs. They could have helped Wilbur strengthen his thumb by offering more genuine encouragement and helpful support to strengthen his will, instead of criticizing and comparing him to his larger thumbed brothers. With regard to that house of straw, his brothers built it for him. They had hoped that he wouldn't end up on their doorsteps, but little thumbed pigs are especially vulnerable to big bad wolves and you know the rest of that story.

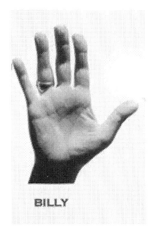

BILLY

Unlike his tiny thumbed brother, Billy had medium sized; medium set column-like thumbs. He was practical, reliable, and responsible. His square fingertips on flexible (not supple, not stiff) fingers, symbolized Billy's need to be orderly and systematic. He was a practical problem solver, planning eventually to go out and get a job working for someone else. Billy did well enough in school, but he was easily satisfied with not asking enough of himself. Billy learned a trade and became a wood worker. That's why Billy built his house from sticks. He wanted logs, but couldn't afford them, so he decided he would build log additions on as time went on.

As a loyal friend, Billy attracted other practical and responsible friends. Billy maintained a small savings account and had some credit card debt, but always made payments on time. Annoyed by his small thumbed brother's irresponsible attitude, Billy gave Wilbur handouts while lecturing him on taking responsibility for his future. Billy had a sowfriend whom he intended to marry, but were waiting until their nest egg was more substantial. What a shame the wolf blew Billy's house down, but rest assured this little piggy started over, building his home more substantially the next time.

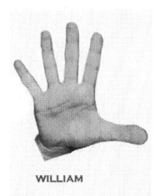

WILLIAM

Everyone thought William (big thumbed brother) was the luckiest pig. He was lucky to have such strong thumbs. They were broad, strong, resilient, low set, and had spatulate tips. William was ambitious and hard working. He was practical like Billy, but he was also independent and very inventive. Always knowing he was going to work for himself, William excelled both academically and athletically. He became president of the student council. All the sows adored him, but

William had his eye on the captain of the cheerleading team. They dated for a few months and then got married. When William graduated from high school, he went straight into business school. His MBA completed, this little piggy went to market with his own general contracting business. While William hired Billy occasionally as a carpenter, he never offered him a full time job because he didn't want Billy to become dependent on him. Wilbur frequently showed up for handouts. William was non-judgmental and generous, but always asked Wilbur to help move something heavy, wash the car, or clean the house. This worked much better than a lecture to keep handouts to a minimum. The wolf was no match for this determined little pig who knew that his well-built house could withstand a hurricane.

By the way, Big Bad the Wolf (Scorpio) had large, high-set clubbed thumbs. These thumbs were hereditary and symbolized a family history of murdering little pigs. Big Bad was obstinate and known for having explosive reactions in difficult situations. Fortunately for the large thumbed pig, the wolf was narrow-minded, unlike his cousin, Clever Fox with his slim waisted paddle-like thumbs. Big Bad hyperventilated, passed out, and died of a head injury while trying to blow down William's reinforced concrete block wall.

Will Power (part 3)
The Murderer's Thumb

The club thumb is known in palmistry books as the "murderer's thumb". I've examined the hands of many murderers (criminally insane) and have seen one club thumb among them. A violent act committed by a club-thumbed person is rarely premeditated. It's an act of uncontrollable rage and unbridled passion. It symbolizes an inflexible nature, with potentially explosive results in difficult situations. Loving and peaceful individuals can also have club thumbs.

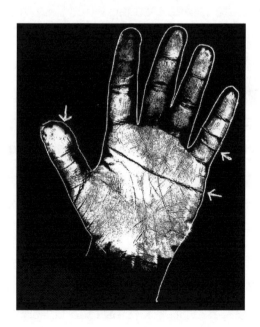

Early in my career, I examined a set of hands with two club thumbs, a simian line on the dominant hand (head and heart line combined) and four phalanges (instead of three) on the little finger of the dominant hand. I thought about what to say to my client. His simian line symbolized a constant battle between head and heart, an inability to verbalize feelings, tremendous focus of energy in the moment, eternal restlessness, and constant soul searching. I didn't have a clue what the four phalanges on the little finger stood for.

I decided to stick my toe in the water before jumping in. "I wouldn't want to make you angry at me" I said cautiously. *"Oh, I never get angry. You can ask anyone. I'm the nicest person in the world".* That's incredible, I thought. "You must be a very evolved person to have overcome the obstacles I see in your hands," I said. He agreed that he was very evolved. I didn't have to be a palmist to see that he was literally repressing a ton of rage. Larger in circumference than he was tall, he had to turn sideways to get through my door. I cautiously explained the challenging implications of what I saw as the dark side of his symbolism. His response was total shock and disbelief. Avoiding the subject of rage was the best path to take from that point on. The rest of our time was spent discussing his creativity, healing abilities, and spirituality. I came to understand in hindsight that his unique pinky represented deafness in one ear (hearing attributed to pinky) and abuse in early childhood (pinky is related to sexuality). His sexually perverted uncle was molesting him, while his weak and ineffectual mother was pretending not to notice.

My ignorance and inexperience made me squirm. I felt relieved when he left. Six months later, he called *"You know, you were right about me. I wasn't ready to hear it. I do have a lot of rage. As a matter of fact, I can kill with thoughts. No really, I really can kill with thoughts. Can I come see you again?"* "I don't really think I can help you," I told him. "Perhaps a psychotherapist is a better choice." He said he planned to see a shrink, but wanted to connect with me first since I stimulated his awareness. I continued to see him for several years after that. Having lost several hundred pounds, he was in his first intimate relationship. This set of hands was destined for a lifetime of obstacles and conflicts about 'right thinking' and 'right use of will power'.

Will Power (part 4)

Thumb Generalities

How is your thumb set on your hand? Is it high, medium, or low set? Higher set thumbs like Wilbur's indicate less adaptable minds that are cautious, reticent to think critically, and self-centered. Frequently carried close to the hand, high set thumbs show a lack of trust, unresponsiveness, and secretiveness.

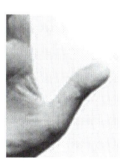

Medium set thumbed individuals like Billy are balanced, sensible, and reasonable. Hard working and dependable, these folk set achievable goals and methodically chip away at them. They're steady workers and reliable friends.

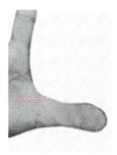

Low set thumbs belong to generous, independent, and freedom loving individuals. Very low set thumbs like William's belong to a rebel who looks for an underdog to support. They give others freedom and they need their own.

Have you seen a thumb that's thick and shapeless like the end of a piece of sausage? What does your common sense tell you? Is he or she reasonable, tactful, diplomatic, and refined? Usually coarse, tactless, and dense, they lack mental agility, and tend to be crude in their reasoning and passions. Most people with sausage-like thumbs do what they want regardless of what others think or feel.

What about a broad well shaped thumb? These strong and determined individuals have abundant physical energy and stamina. They can be aggressive and blunt. What about a thumb that's shapely and column-like in appearance? Strong will, tact, and refinement rule the person. What if the thumb looks like a paddle with a broad tip and a waisted (narrowing at center) second phalanx? There's a lot of determination, backed up with strong tact and diplomacy. These folk can persuade others with refined logic. What if the tip of a thumb looks as though it was smashed or flattened? This is the 'nervous' thumb, indicating a nervous temperament and lack of balanced energy.

Let's consider the shape of the tip of the thumb. The four most common shapes are conical, round, square, and spatulate. The conical thumb (Wilbur) is cone-like in appearance. It belongs to an idealistic, impulsive, and impressionable individual who loves beauty and backs down in confrontation because will is softened by a conical tip.

A round tip balances idealism and practicality. Square tips (Billy) are most practical of all tips. Square adds common sense, reliability, and dependability. A spatulate tip (William) belongs to a strong willed action-oriented individual who loves his independence, originality, and unconventionality. Sometimes, you'll see pointed fingertips. Relatively rare, they indicate a highly sensitive and impractical nature. When a person's headline dips down into the heel of the hand, the person may have some psychic abilities, though they may not be aware of it.

Is a thumb stiff? Slightly flexible? Highly flexible? Very stiff thumbs feel like they'll break before they bend. Stiff thumbs represent stubborn, persistent, determined individuals who may also be cautious, economical, and resolute. Some of the nastiest stiff-thumbed habits are possessiveness and jealousy that cause unnecessary suffering. Supple thumbed people (like Wilbur) are adaptable, sympathetic, generous, and versatile. They love being extreme, outrageous, and extravagant. They'd make great philanthropists, if they could only figure out how to hold on to money. They ask too little for themselves and haven't learned how to say "no." Distractions are normal for supple thumbs. Frequently spreading themselves too thin, they become the proverbial "jack of all trades, master of none". I encourage supple thumbed people to embrace focus, discipline, and structure. It's like prescribing bad tasting medicine for them. Many people with highly flexible thumbs, fingers, and hands have spent their life resenting obligation, avoiding responsibility, rebelling against authority, living in fantasy, self-medicating, or hopefully adapting to their obligations and responsibilities.

Health

VERTICAL   WHITE   BEAU'S   IRON
LINES   FLECKS   LINES   DEFICIENCY

In the days before computerized medical diagnosis, doctors used their intuition, tasted a patient's urine, looked into their eyes, inspected their tongue, and examined their hands to diagnose illness. Dozens of illnesses can be diagnosed from fingernails alone, which are considered windows to a person's health. Some health problems which can be diagnosed by examining the nails are: anemia, malnutrition, thyroid disease, diseases of the liver, heart, lungs, and colon, chronic respiratory disease, lymphatic problems, diabetes, carpal tunnel syndrome, Raynaud's disease, high blood pressure, psoriasis, eczema, rheumatoid arthritis, ulcers, sickle cell anemia, and Hodgkin's disease. Many stress related diseases and some cancers can be detected in fingerprints and skin ridge patterns (dermatoglyphics). Lines in the hands can indicate conditions of the heart, brain, kidneys, liver, stomach, and sexual systems.

I always ask female clients before coming for a private consultation to remove their nail polish so that I can observe the color and texture of their nails, protecting the delicate nerve centers in their fingertips. When nerve centers are operating in a healthy way, nails appear smooth textured, pink, and clear. When nerve centers are impaired, this leaves an impression on the nail texture and color that must be read accordingly. A very fine and healthy person will tend to have fine and healthy nails, while a coarse person will have coarse or fluted (vertical ridges) nails. The more the nails appear to be fluted, the more the nervous system is affected. Fluting naturally occurs more with aging. People with Type **A** personalities tend to have large moons. Small moons are normal, while I've found that no moons often correspond to low blood pressure or slower metabolism.

Stress depletes calcium in the body, which shows up in the form of white flecks in the nails. Wherever you see flecks, apply both a time and stress factor to the meaning of that particular finger. A nail takes approximately six months to grow out. If you see white flecks in the middle of the nail on a person's middle finger, it's likely that three months ago they may have experienced a stressful situation in their career or work. If the white fleck is on the very tip of the index finger, then about six months ago, they may have experienced a blow to their self-esteem.

I'm not a medical palmist. If I see a serious potential health problem, I'm always careful not to alarm my client. I suggest that they consult their doctor. Most health challenges are natural predispositions of specific character types. By understanding types will help you understand corresponding health challenges. People with square palms and long fingers (Thinking) can have problems with their nervous system, bronchial system, thyroid gland, issues with memory loss, headaches, speech impediments, and respiratory difficulties. Square palms and short fingers (Practical) may struggle with skin, teeth, knees, ligaments, deafness, rheumatism, gout, paralysis, hardening of the arteries, hemorrhoids, and varicose veins.

Individuals with rectangular palms and short fingers (Intuitive) are generally healthy types, but prone to blood disorders, liver trouble, diabetes, stroke, high blood pressure, heart failure, and problems with hips, thighs, and throat. Many challenges result from overindulging in food and drink. People with rectangular palms and long fingers (Feeling) have stomach and colon problems, reproductive issues, venereal diseases, challenges with bodily fluids, and foot problems. Health will be covered in more depth in the future when we get to the stories.

Relationships

Relationships are my all-time favorite application of palmistry. Counseling couples is challenging because many couples can't see or don't want to see their issues. Choosing safe is a whole lot easier than choosing satisfying for one or both of them. A competent palmist can instantly see where compromise is possible and where it's not. A couple may not be ready to face the unvarnished truth of their partnership.

I remember one woman with square hands and long slender very flexible fingers (Thinking) who I read at an event. As I examined her hands, she told me "she was so very happy" because she had "the best husband in the world."

She was certainly beautiful looking, however, her hands told another tale of Sleeping Beauty, waiting for her prince to awaken her. Her very supple thumbs, inwardly curving pinky finger, and the end of her heart line dipping down to touch her headline indicated to me that she was living in a fantasy world of avoiding confrontation. Instead of shining light on what needed to be seen, she subconsciously rationalized and compartmentalized her feelings while she adapted to undesirable circumstances. She was desperately trying to be a person she thought her husband wanted and needed her to be. An overcritical and controlling father had been physically or emotionally absent during her formative years. She was programmed to "act nice", help make peace, and try to make everyone happy. "Be yourself", I advised.

A few moments later, her Prince Charming sat down. His rectangular palms and short flexible fingers (Intuitive), indicated that he was her polar opposite, but not necessarily incompatible. She was a trophy, an object he had won by becoming wealthy. He told me he was having an affair with another woman and was thinking of leaving his wife.

Astonished, I asked why he hadn't informed her of his feelings. "It's impossible. She sees what she wants to see. I'm guilty for deceiving her and angry for having to. I've lost respect for both of us. Betraying her naïve trust makes me hate myself."

"Tell her the truth", I suggested.

It appears that Sleeping Beauty was soon to be rudely awakened. She and her Prince Charming might not been in this predicament had they recognized their issues before they got married. If only they had known how to look at their hands while they lovingly held each other's.

That same evening, another couple sat down. She had long small very flexible hands, short fingers, and smooth joints (Intuitive) He had very stiff hands with long knotty fingers.

He was a control freak. She was a freedom lover. He was extremely practical and methodical. She was creative and spontaneous. His jealousy and possessiveness would eventually drive her nuts. They sat soberly while I spoke about compromise, trust, and learning to partner more and better.

The rest of the evening, he became my shadow, a walking testimonial, saying to everyone, "My wife loves this guy."

At the end of the party, his wife came up and said to me, "You might have helped save our marriage".

Marriage

When I was thirty-eight years old I married Joanna, a twenty-six year old dancer. Astrologically, Joanna has an Aries sun, Gemini moon, and Taurus rising. Her square palms, widely spread fingers, low-set stiff-thumb, and head and life line connected at their beginning harmoniously blend her sun, moon, and rising sign, symbolizing the personification of rebellious stubbornness. I call her "Ram-Bull".

I have a Gemini Sun, Taurus moon, and Scorpio rising. My square palms and widely spread long fingers reveal the sometimes embarrassing versatility of my very flexible hands and nature. Joanna calls me "a piece of work in progress." She's twelve years younger, which makes us 'the boars' at Chinese New Year's parties.

Before I asked Joanna to marry me, I took a close look at her hands. Traditionally, most palmists look for conformation of marriage in three places in the hands: horizontal lines under the pinky finger, lines touching the life line within the ball of the thumb, and lines connecting to or branching from the fate line. This is a nebulous area of palmistry; marriage can be difficult to judge in terms of detail and timing. Joanna had one horizontal line under her pinky that indicated to me that she would commit to a life partner in her mid-thirties.

I considered that maybe our timing was off and said so, "Your hands say that you won't be ready to fully commit to a life partner until your mid-thirties." She let me know that palmistry was wrong and I was up to my eyeballs in bullshit.

We married despite palmistry. When Joanna was thirty-three and I was forty-five, Cassie was born. We team worked like never before to become the best parents we could be. When Cassie was two years old, Joanna said to me, "Do you remember when you told me that I wouldn't truly commit to a soul mate until I was in my mid-thirties and I said you were crazy?" I nodded. "You were right."

Palmistry doesn't always show external events as accurately as symbolizing internal changes. Marriage preferences, propensities, and potentials will be discussed in depth when we get to individual character types. Speaking of nebulous areas of palmistry, our daughter Cassie didn't appear in my hands until after she was born.

Creativity

"The worst enemy of creativity is self-doubt" Sylvia Plath

Clients say, "I'm not creative." "I don't have a creative bone in my body." "I can't draw a straight line if my life depended on it." Many people think that being creative is being artistic. They ask, "How can I be more creative?" I encourage using their imagination, being original, thinking critically, and viewing creativity not as a goal, but as an innate birthright.

People agree that creativity is a good thing to have, though few can effectively define it. Scientists try to measure our C.Q.s along with our I.Q.s. Neurologists designate the frontal lobe of the cerebral cortex of our brain as the location for creativity. Creativity and hands are inextricably linked. Hands may be a small body part, but they occupy a huge space in our cerebral cortex. As we solve problems, our hands carry out the messages of our minds, and as they do the work, they're topographically mapping our motivations, character, behavior, values, thinking, feelings, will power, health, relationships, philosophy, purpose, hopes, and fears.

Creativity is like the bastard prodigal child of great joy and intense suffering. Researchers agree that creativity thrives in extremes and opposites. It can sprout in brilliant light or total darkness, blossom in absolute good or the darkest evil, and flourish in razor sharp focus or complete distraction. Western mythology links creativity, sex, death, and transformation. Like us, creativity is born, procreates, and dies.

Creativity produces art and music that pulls our heartstrings, ignites our spirits, inspires us, and fills us with joy, passion, and desire. Creativity within science has enabled us to have a very high standard of living by heating our homes and allowing us to travel and communicate freely. Creativity triumphs over any and all obstacles. When our creative juices are flowing, we can embrace our creative processes, take creative license, and do anything but steal someone else's creativity. When our work is done, there's recreation.

Let's explore the dark side of creativity. Creativity manifests darkly in many ways by avoiding what we know is right and compartmentalizing, analyzing, and rationalizing unhealthy thoughts and feelings. Temptation germinates the seeds of the shameful secrets that nourish guilt, rob honesty, compromise integrity, and tarnish nobility. Fear debilitates, sabotages, and betrays us. It takes a lot of creativity and a good memory to juggle promises, lies, and excuses. Some of the symptoms of dark creativity are: "I may have not told the whole truth, but I didn't lie." "I didn't mean to tell." "I never intended to hurt anyone." "The temptation was too strong." "Sorry for my part."

In order to create, a symbolic death must take place. Letting go, no matter how painful, creates space for new choices, actions, and circumstances. I know a lot about death and creativity. Pluto rules my horoscope. Pluto, Scorpio, and the eighth house symbolize transformation in astrology. Catastrophic business and personal losses forced me to rethink, restructure, and recreate my life several times. Pluto is master of the 'little death' (sexual orgasm). He welcomes us as executioner, coroner, and mortician at our final exit.

 Voldemort, Darth Vader, the Mummy, and the Big Bad Wolf are modern Plutonian types.

Reading hands is more about quality than quantity. We can't see the extent of creativity in our hands, but we can see the qualities of creativity.

Creative orientation can be observed in the shapes and proportions of our hands. Our desire to create is revealed by the conditions and qualities of our thumb and index finger. Ways we structure and communicate our creativity can be seen in the middle and pinky fingers. How we express creativity is mirrored in the elasticity, consistency, color, texture, and flexibility of hands and fingers. Our imagination is incarnate in the qualities and directions of our head line. Our appreciation of art, music, nature, kids, food, home, etc., can be seen in the combo of ball of thumb and ring finger.

The length of a lifeline does not determine the length of life. No one can or should tell you when you will die. That's God's job. Your job is to be personally and collectively creative in as constructive (as opposed to destructive) ways as possible. Positive creativity is essential to our good health and the good health of our world.

Perception

"Do Homosexuals have shorter index fingers than ring fingers?"

According to a full-page article entitled "FINGERS TIP OFF HOMOSEXUALITY" first published in the New York Post on March 30, 2,000 the answer is **"Yes"**. Researchers at the University of California at Berkley surveyed 720 gay men at street fairs in San Francisco and determined that gay men had shorter index fingers than heterosexual men. In a second article on March 31st, the Post claimed this was *"the most talked about story in the history of the New York Post"*.

The study explained how larger amounts of male hormones in Mom's womb linked short index fingers to gays. The theory also extended to ring fingers, *"Homosexuals and lesbians have shorter index fingers than ring fingers."*

Predicting someone is gay from the length of his or her index finger is absurd. Sexual proclivities and appetites in general are reflected in the shapes, proportions, flexibility, elasticity, consistency, and colors of the hands and fingers. Sexual behavior including seductiveness, passive/aggressiveness, and fetishes are reflected in the ball of the thumb, heart line, and pinky finger. Index fingers do not provide answers to questions of sexual orientation. I've examined many thousands of long-index-fingered gays and short-index-fingered straights at special events. A predominance of photographers, designers, architects, craftsmen, actors, performers, teachers, and salespeople has longer ring than index fingers.

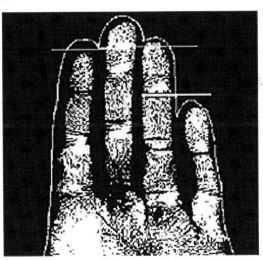

Your index finger does say a lot about your character. Here is the long and short of index fingers. A short index fingered person (less than half way to the middle of the top phalange of the middle finger), will have to work harder to achieve his or her goals than the long-index-fingered person. His major challenge is learning to value himself enough, to ask for what he's worth. Too many short-index-fingered people received too little emotional support and encouragement while growing up. They were unable to be their authentic selves.

Plenty of successful individuals have short index fingers; however, nothing came easily to them. They earned every drop of whatever they achieved. What the Berkley survey is saying, but doesn't realize, is that the particular focus group of gay people they found at street fairs battle with issues of self-esteem. Perhaps a parent was physically or emotionally unavailable during their formative years. It's no wonder so many gay people have short index fingers considering how confused, afraid, angry, and perverse western culture is concerning homosexuality.

I chose Mitt Romney to draw attention to and dispel one of many myths about palmistry. You can assume that Barack Obama, Bill Clinton, and George Bush are also gay or bi as they have longer ring fingers than index fingers. The "digit ratio theory" doesn't define homosexuality, but it does perpetuate stereotypes and prejudices in our culture.

Purpose

If a man hasn't discovered something that he will die for, he isn't fit to live."

Martin Luther King Jr.

Each of us has a role to perform on this stage of life; our hands reveal the plot. Whether we're performing our destined role or not, our hands reveal the truth of who we are. Palmistry is a lens through which we can observe ourselves and others from the outside in. In my role as five-minute fortuneteller at special events, I often read whole groups of people who have made major life choices that work externally but not internally. Many people are doing what they think they *should* or *are supposed to* be doing.

I've met engineers who'd be happier psychologists, lawyers who'd be more fulfilled as writers, doctors barely aware of other potentials, and countless individuals from all walks of life who for one reason or another haven't valued their natural gifts or embraced their innate talents and abilities.

For five years in a row, I examined hands of incoming students at freshman orientation for the Asian Studies department at Columbia University. Cultural paradigms influenced many Asian American students who told me their families never encouraged their creativity and talents. For practical or social reasons, their natural gifts were not a priority. I advised and encouraged these young adults to nourish their latent talents by choosing satisfying and fulfilling interests and hobbies.

One of the comments I often hear is *"My hands are the way they are because of what I do"* referring to hand size and shape, and whether they are hard or soft, rough or smooth, or callused. That's not true. Your hands reflect what you were designed to do.

It's important to recognize that what we do is not who we are. Character, motivations, abilities, and talents can be seen in the size, shape, and proportions of hands.

This is worth repeating many times. There are four basic archetypes: Intuitive, Practical, Thinking, and Feeling. One of these four types dominates our personal psyche. Finger lengths and proportions, tips, knots, and nails, reveal how we relate to others and manifest our potentials in the world around us. Texture, color, and elasticity of skin, along with the flexibility and consistency of hands reveal how we adapt to change. Our lines and gestures provide more detailed information about our life choices and circumstances. The arts and crafts of interpretation and counseling are learned and absorbed over time with study and practice.

Spirituality

"Science without religion is lame, religion without science is blind." Albert Einstein

Clients ask, "Do you think I'm a spiritual person?"
"Do I have a line in my hand that shows spirituality?"
"How can I become more spiritual?" I ask, "What does spirituality mean to you?"

Spirituality is subjective. Everyone agrees that spirituality is a good thing to have, though few can effectively define it. To the ancients, spirituality was life, not in its physical aspect, but as a universal principle that infuses, drives, and sustains existence. It was an abstract energy in man that is the only reality in the midst of an ever-changing world.

Hermes, western mythology's father of communication and wisdom, described spirit as the essence that permeates and the glue that connects everything. Our spiritual development is dependent on recognizing, realizing, and manifesting the spirit within us.

To an eastern philosopher, spirit is universal. It's never individualized. One person does not have one spirit and another person another. Man is a race of spiritually indivisible individuals. There are no divine spirits, human spirits, animal spirits, or plant spirits, but one spirit flowing through all divine forms. Chinese Taoists say, "As springs flow into streams, streams into rivers, and rivers into oceans, evolution is imprisoned in all things flowing through innumerable forms back to the sea of its own universality".

In all esoteric teachings, the goal of spirituality is about raising consciousness in order to become aware of something greater, higher, and deeper than things appear to be in the moment. We reference all that is good, exalting, uplifting, and god-like in man's nature. A feeling of reverence, devotion, attention, and a separation from all that's low and degrading is present.

Manly Hall postulates in his book, Questions and Answers: Fundamentals of the Esoteric Sciences, "All men suffer from certain reasonable doubts concerning life and truth. Spirituality is not in keeping with either the church or state. Each person is his own high priest and the obligations he makes to himself are what's real."

Rudolf Steiner, in his book, <u>Knowledge of Higher Worlds and its Attainment</u>, explains that human beings can attain spiritual enlightenment and wisdom through diligent esoteric study. The primary goal of this study is to recognize a life of truth and inner tranquility. There are six attributes that initiates strive to acquire: control of thought, control of actions, tolerance (towards persons, creatures, and circumstances), impartiality (the faith which can move mountains), equanimity (cultivation of inner balance), and perseverance.

Many people have a concept of spirituality that is colored by the exoteric and dogmatic beliefs of formalized religion. For example, you can become more spiritual by being celibate, denying materiality, or fasting. These are ideologies fostered by religious institutions in order to further their own private agendas. Modern psychologists believe that while consciously denying something, the surrounding issues become highly charged.

Edward Whitmont, in The Symbolic Quest, writes, "Whatever is repressed while then lost in consciousness still does not disappear. It becomes an unconscious compulsive force, which then has primitive and potentially destructive characteristics.

Knowledge without wisdom is lame, religion without spirituality is blind. No wonder so many priests are sexual predators. I've examined the hands of many violent criminals who discovered religion while they were incarcerated. Few were in touch with their spirituality.

Spirituality connects anyone and everything in all time and every place. When I look for spirituality in the hands, I hope to find a firm handshake, pink elastic skin, and a full ball of thumb that embraces life with enthusiasm and appreciation. Within the ball of thumb are lines parallel to the lifeline. These lines indicate an ability to have intimacy with others. More and longer lines reveal more and longer intimacies. Even one line is good, however, because it shows that a person is able to have intimacy with another person.

William Benham (father of western palmistry) had an electric current theory of lines. He believed that current from the brain etches the lines in the hands, which in turn, reflect the qualities and directions of the person's thoughts, intentions, and actions. Clear deep lines allow the current to flow freely. Frayed or islanded lines are produced by and represent interruptions and disruptions in the life force. Sometimes there is confusion at the beginning of a line and clarity over time. Many people become conscious of their struggles and thrive as they age despite challenging childhoods full of difficult obstacles. They become more spiritual over time, which is reflected in their hands.

Fingerprints also influence spirituality. People with whorl fingerprints rarely accept religious dogma and preconceived ideologies. They're attracted to more unconventional and original philosophies. That's especially true on the index finger. Loops are social and adaptable. You'll find loops in all religions because a majority of people has some. Arch prints reflect more social conditioning and conventional religious beliefs. No matter what a person's hands say, no one is really able to comprehend the essence of another person's spirituality until they have a dialogue with the person.

Early in my palmistry career, I was invited to attend a spiritual event for Swami Ji, a holy man, who arrived from India to tour the United States. Many followers flocked to his northeast talk in upstate New York to receive his wisdom and blessings. After the event, I got to spend quality private time with him. It was my first experience with a guru. I was surprised by how many mundane questions he asked me as I examined his hands, about his competition, finances, and (it seemed to me) petty concerns about his immediate staff and personal comfort. We examined ways in which his outer worldly concerns challenged his inner-world.

Every person has material and spiritual concerns and questions. I wouldn't presume to tell anyone they weren't spiritual. Everyone is spiritual by degree. People frequently tell me how spiritual they are. I'm often surprised when I examine their hands to discover how very closed or rigid they are in their ideologies and attitudes.

I refuse to argue with fundamentalists about anything, but I do sprinkle seeds of spiritual thought and encourage them to sprout. Everyone must eventually learn to weed, prune, and fertilize his or her spiritual garden.

As the human race relentlessly races against bad shit happening, many more people are becoming more spiritual. We grow more aware of our spirituality as we realize our impending mortality. I just look in the mirror.

AIDS was a death sentence in the late 1980's. Spirituality blossomed as people suffered and died. In the 21st century, our immune deficient environment, ailing economy, broken healthcare system, decaying infrastructure, partisan political system, fundamentalist religious ideologies, and terrorism, etc. are driving people to seek answers within themselves. No matter what any of us thinks about his or her spirituality, priceless inner treasure is patiently waiting to be discovered at the ends of our arms.

Children

Most parents want to be good parents. I frequently hear young parents saying, "I'm not going to make the same mistakes on my kids as my parents made on me." While they may not make the same mistakes as their parents, they'll make other mistakes. As my friend and fellow astrologer, Michael Lutin, jokingly quips, "It's easy to forgive your parents after you screwed up your own kids."

Over twenty years ago, I observed hundreds of criminally insane people's hands while working two days a week over a two-year period in the rehab department of a forensic psychiatric hospital. I was amazed how many of them were named Hope, Faith, Angel, Jesus, Grace, Joy, and Mary by highly dysfunctional role models who hoped that god would bless and help them with their child. Sadly, many of those parents ended up physically and emotionally abusing their kids until god's blessings transformed into acts of violence that finally landed their children in maximum-security forensic mental hospitals for the criminally insane.

Learning to read your kid's hands is the best way to tailor your parenting to the individual character of each child. Knowing your child's character will place your own needs as well as your child's needs under a microscope. No matter what the age of your child, palmistry can help you to understand his or her real needs and concerns.

You'll learn to be more patient and tolerant by observing your child's hands. As you realize your children's natural potentials, talents, abilities, and challenges, you can encourage the best in them, help create a meaningful educational plan, and point them in the direction of a fulfilling career and life.

 I was able to participate in the delivery of my child at birth. I pulled her from my wife's womb and cut her umbilical cord. Joanna tells the story of how I was reading our baby's hands before knowing what sex she was. It's true. Her little hands could barely wrap around my index finger and they already had a story to tell. Her character was sculpted in the shape and proportions of her hands; her strengths and weaknesses, talents, goals, and dreams engraved in her palms. Those tiny hands were beautiful, but on closer inspection, I felt somewhat confused. Joanna and I have such long heart lines (romantic, sentimental, and very much able and wanting to express our feelings) and our daughter's heart line was so short (emotionally serious, untrusting, and unable to verbalize feelings). In addition, her index finger was very short which symbolized future problems with self-esteem and spirituality. During her first two years of life, she was very cautious, fearful, untrusting, and extremely clingy.

Armed with foresight, Joanna, and I nourished and encouraged her to unfold as who she wanted and needed to be. Based on our decision and commitment, along with Cassie's tremendous will power and determination, her index finger and heart line grew longer during her formative years.

Now, at twenty-two, she's self-assured, fiercely independent, healthy, and although still an emotionally serious person, she's able to express her true feelings.

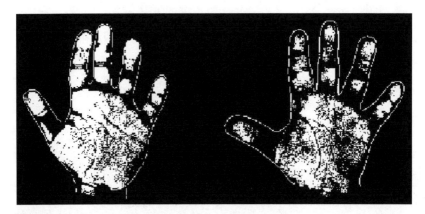

Children's hands change dramatically during the first five years of life. It's no surprise that psychologists call this period the "formative years". One of the best examples I've seen of changes in a child's hands was illustrated in Andrew Fitzherbert's book, Hand Psychology. My friend and fellow palmist, Marion Gale gave me permission to use the above prints and copy. These are her prints of the same child. On the left, at age two, he's an orphan, having lost both parents. Notice the curved index finger and widely spaced low set pinky finger. There's a lot of fear and insecurity in this hand. On the right, at age seven, five years after loving relatives have taken him in and cared for him, he has a confident hand with a strong and straight index finger and a healthy pinky finger. The primary lines in his hands strengthened while unnecessary peripheral lines disappeared.

Palmistry and Astrology

Tens of millions of people read their horoscopes daily in newspapers and magazines without realizing the true value of astrology. More ancient than the pyramids, astrology is a science and art that examines relationships between the cycles of celestial bodies and life on earth. Astronomical patterns synchronize with life experience and personality patterns. Every moment in time and space has an exclusive signature. A natal horoscope is a unique map of the positions of planets in the heavens at a time and place of a birth. Kings, Presidents, Dictators, Philosophers, Mystics, and Scholars throughout history have used astrology (and still do) to understand and influence world events.

I studied astrology for several years before I began learning palmistry. Initially, I found astrology to be very complex and mathematical, however, with practice I began to recognize a profoundly simple and elegant system for examining human nature, patterns, timing, and life cycles. One problem with Astrology for me is that accurate forecasting is an exacting science. I know from personal experience that most doctors, nurses, and parents are not watching the clock at a baby's first breath. Clients often give birth times on the hour or half hour. Many clients don't know whether they were born in the morning or evening. Others depend on a vague memory of their mother long after the event. My mother wanted to have natural childbirth, however, after 24 hours in labor; the obstetrician finally cut me out in order to save her life. Mom believed that she remembered my birth time correctly, but her memory was different from my original birth certificate, which I ended up using to construct my horoscope.

One more thing that I discovered by reading hands was that even when a birth time is correct, it doesn't mean that a natal horoscope reveals the whole picture. In astrology, the ascendant (rising sign) of the natal horoscope is considered the basis for determining behavior, however, I discovered from reading hands that a person's sun or moon or powerful aspects between planets or perhaps a stellium (a grouping of three or four) of planets in a particular house might actually be dominating their personality.

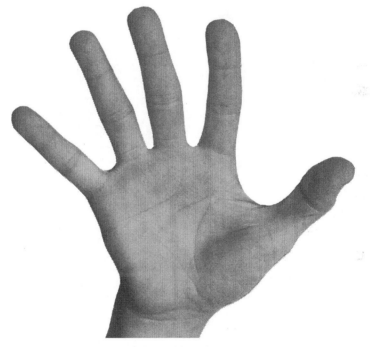

I have Scorpio rising, Saturn conjunct Pluto straddling my Leo Midheaven, and a stellium of Gemini planets (4) in my 8th house. You'd think my hands would be very Scorpio, but instead they're very Gemini. That's not to say that I'm not Plutonian. I am, but not in the ways I behave. Sometimes, clients are different than I expect they'll be from looking at their horoscope. Imagine their chart is dominated by mutable water or air without a drop of earth. I'm expecting them to float through the door. Instead, a much grounded person walks in. When I look at their hands, I see no mutability, air, or water. Their astrology begins to make more sense after I see how they've compensated for whatever they lack in their astrological symbolism. I've learned not to depend on a person's horoscope to observe their character. Learning palmistry and astrology have helped me to understand both better. Astrology is especially helpful in confirming and affirming what I already see in a person's hands. It also provides additional information about their behavioral patterns, timing, and life cycles.

I've applied an astrological framework to palmistry to help identify and define twelve basic character types. Western astrology and palmistry share the same Greek and Roman gods. Their family relationships are forever being acted out in our lives. Humanity is one huge dysfunctional family and each of us is a member. I've introduced astrology's four elements in palmistry as psychological types: Fire (Intuitive), Earth (Practical), Air (Thinking), and Water (Feeling).

Four Basic Archetypes

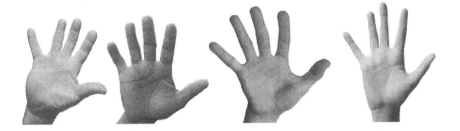

INTUITIVE	PRACTICAL	**THINKING**	**FEELING**
Long Palm	Square Palm	Square Palm	Long Palm
Short Fingers	Short Fingers	Long Fingers	Long Fingers

Shapes and proportions of hands reveal one of four basic personality types.

INTUITIVE or PRACTICAL qualities dominate when fingers are shorter than palms. Intuitive types with their long palms and short fingers take chances when inspired. Practical types with square palms and short fingers are logical, methodical, pragmatic, and make decisions based on objective reality.

THINKING or FEELING qualities dominate when fingers are longer than palms. Thinking types with square palms and long fingers must learn not to spread themselves too thin. Feeling types with long palms and long fingers must learn to trust their feelings in order to trust and be comfortable with others.

Reading hands is like a Meyers Briggs personality test incarnate. Large hands enjoy detail and organization. Small hands detest detail, are conceptual, and love big ideas. Small-handed folk need to delegate the detail work to their large handed brethren.

Speaking of details, every detail needs to be examined in the context of the whole and all other details at the same time. The danger in interpreting details out of context is in substituting one form of pre-determinism for another by reducing individuality to cookbook formulas. Most palmistry books do that. Every detail has meaning (even rings, scars, warts and birthmarks). Until you have determined the basic hand type, all details are superficial. The meaning of any detail can change depending on the question asked and the character of the individual. No matter our circumstances, we still have plenty of free will to exercise our thinking, feelings, and actions. We cannot alter the past, but we can change our present and influence our futures.

Intuitive Type

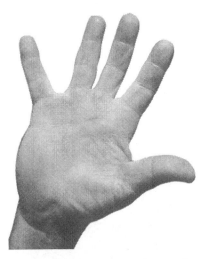

The Intuitive archetype has rectangular palms and short fingers. These highly spirited, enthusiastic individuals dislike details, need to grasp the whole picture, pride themselves on their honesty, and require a lot of freedom to express themselves naturally. They're extroverted, very busy, objective, independent thinkers who must learn to set goals in order to accomplish their objectives. Easily bored when life gets mundane or routine, Intuitive types need to stay inspired and passionate while cultivating clear vision and enduring patience. They're frequently accused of being opinionated because their point of view is so imperative. Communicating clearly and effectively is a must.

The best way for Intuitive types to flourish and blossom is to behave responsibly and naturally in their relationships and creative self-expression. Intuitive types can be broken down into three modalities and character types: **Pioneers** *initiate*, **Actors** maintain, and **Wanderers** adapt.

"The most difficult job in the world is not being president. It's being a parent." Former President Bill Clinton is an Intuitive type. He's an **Actor**. Born three months after his real dad died, Bill was raised by an abusive alcoholic stepfather. Many **Actors** spend much of their lives searching for approval from father figures because their own fathers were physically or emotionally absent during their formative years. A lifelong quest for an **Actor** is a hero's journey to become a devoted father figure who loves unconditionally and without expectation.

Although people question Bill Clinton's character, Bill is actually true to his character. He's a Sun / Jupiter type, which blends Apollo and Zeus, two of the most powerful, charismatic, and sexiest gods in Greek myth. Bill can rule the free world, have fun, enjoy sex, and play the saxophone, all at the same time. Zeus was famous for his seductions and philandering. Apollo was irresistible. It's not easy to find healthy creative outlets for all that libido.

Many of the most powerful men and women in the world are philanderers with sexual addictions. Excess testosterone comes with the territory. Zeus could have whatever female mortal he wanted. His problem was getting away with it. His wife Hera was famous for kicking his butt by punishing his conquests and their offspring. You can bet Hillary booted Bill's behind when he got caught. It's hard to get away with much when you're a public figure and mortal.

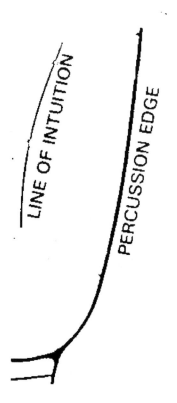

You don't have to be an Intuitive type to be intuitive. Short fingered people in general have a stronger gut level intuition than long fingered folk. People who have conical fingertips and smooth joints on their fingers tend to be more intuitive than people who don't. When the head line dips down toward the heel of the hand, intuition and imagination play a greater role in the person's life. Some people have a line of intuition curving toward the percussion of the hand which also symbolizes a sixth sense. There are dermatoglyphics (skin ridge patterns, which will be discussed later) that indicate enhanced intuition. Of course, by paying attention to and using our intuition, we begin to learn to trust it. I sometimes have accurate and unexplainable insights while examining someone's hands. I chalk that up to having cultivated my intuition over many years.

Practical Type

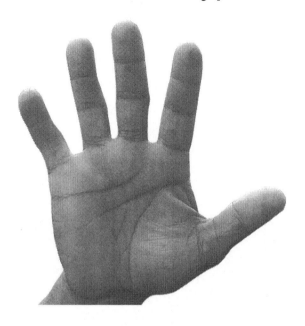

The Practical type has square palms and short fingers. Pure types have very few peripheral lines in their palms, with hardly any interruptions on the three main lines (head, heart, and life). Skin ridge patterns are usually coarser than the other three archetypes. Square shaped fingertips and arch fingerprints are frequently seen, and there's often stiffness in the joints of the fingers and thumb. Practical types are driven by their physical senses. As the most responsible, reliable, dependable, pragmatic and objective of all types, they have an innate understanding of how the material world works. They trust what they can see and feel, not inspirations, ideas or intuitions. As a matter of fact, they tend to get so involved in practical matters, it limits imagination and abstract ability. Because the world of work dominates their life, they need to be careful not to get addicted to routine and order. They love their homes, family, friendships, and food as well as work. This type's biggest challenges are learning to trust their gut, relinquish control, and let go once the handwriting is on the wall. The Practical type is the *Pragmatist* who initiates, the *Objectivist* who maintains, or the *Analyst* who adapts.

Hillary Clinton is a Practical type - a *Pragmatist*. The *Pragmatist* is the most serious and responsible of all types. Hillary is a natural business leader and great manager, able to deal with the responsibility of each and every aspect of daily business while maintaining her long-range vision.

As a structured, disciplined, focused, and dependable leader, she expects you to be on time and do what you say. She has no patience for excuses and doesn't trust slick and flashy types (though she married one). Practical, prudent, and efficient, Hillary patiently bides her time until the right circumstances are present. She's a workaholic who won't think twice about coming in early or staying late when a task needs to be finished. She has a dry sense of humor, and occasionally, a cold and pessimistic dark side.

Hillary's separated head and life line indicates that she's much less conservative than people think. Even though she'd prefer to stray from the rules, she continues to support a system she doesn't know how to change. Hillary is independent and freedom loving; she hates bureaucracy despite working in one and detests critical authority figures. She has an inherent conflict between taking responsibility and having freedom. Good causes inspire and impassion Hillary; unless she has a worthy quest, her life becomes too mundane. She's easily bored, and becomes restless and impatient with routines. Being Secretary of State suited her temperament well. I'll vote for her if she runs for President.

Hillary is not jealous or possessive, but demands too little of her partner in her emotional life (low set pinky finger). She needs to listen more to her natural intuition and less to her handlers. Hillary has less natural charm, but much greater executive abilities than her husband Bill. Unlike Bill, she doesn't need anyone's approval.

You don't have to be a **Practical** type to be practical. Any hand that tends to have a square appearance adds a lot of practicality to the personality. Head lines and heart lines that run straight across the palm without curving are practical. Not having many lines in the hand can help a person to stay focused and resist distraction. A long straight fate line extending from the wrist to under the middle finger symbolizes a 'nose to the grindstone' kind of person. Arch fingerprints tend to enhance practicality – at least in the area that the particular finger represents.

Fingerprints are unchangeable; however, other qualities in hands can change. As a child, my hands were so highly flexible that structure, discipline, and focus seemed impossible. I didn't have a clue how to be practical. I had a hard time realizing it at the time, but fortunately, I had a mother who forced me to be more realistic and eventually (it took almost thirty years) the joints in my conscious hand stiffened up. My unconscious (left) hand is still very flexible.

Thinking Type

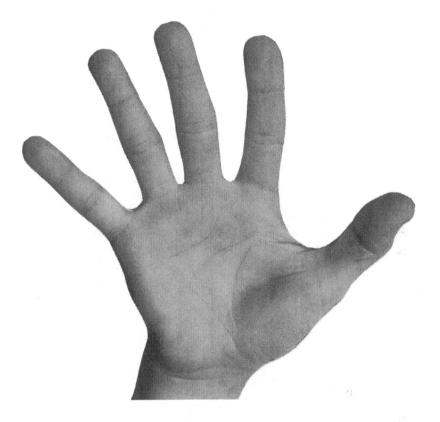

Thinking types have square palms and long fingers, often widely spread. Thinking types are communicators. They love the idea stage of development, before projects materialize. They're frequently accused of being impractical dreamers, but without them, not much new would happen. They can detach themselves from mundane reality and gain objectivity and perspective on almost anything. They're the most social of all types and can see your point of view, even if they don't agree with you. They're capable of dealing with plenty of analysis, detail and information, although they'd rather be unencumbered and free from material realities. On the downside, they tend to overvalue the intellect and play down emotion. They can easily become distracted and scattered and resist focus, discipline and structure. They can also be nervous, restless, superficial, and unreliable. Thinking types feel threatened when their opinions are ignored or challenged without good reason.

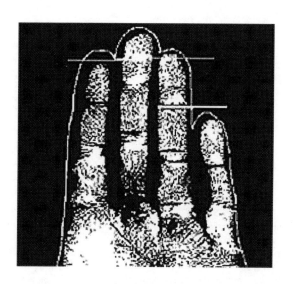

All people have a thinking function. By looking at the pinky finger, we begin to learn more about our thinking. The pinky is normally the shortest finger. When the tip is longer than the crease between the first and second phalange of the ring finger, it's considered long. When it's shorter, it's considered short. Our pinky finger shows our ability to communicate. It also indicates truthfulness. We can see technical, language, family, and sexual issues and potentials in our pinky finger. Our early family dynamic may be observed in the way the pinky is set on the hands. If it's very short or low set, trust is a major issue. Many women who have very low set pinkies have told me that they have trouble having orgasms. The real challenge is having real intimacy.

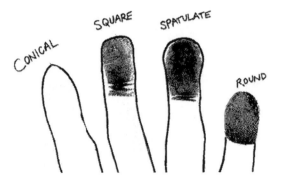

Fingertips also indicate our thinking function. Each finger has three phalanges, divided by two joints in each finger, which may or may not have a developed knot at each. The top phalange represents our thinking. When it is dominant (longer than the other two phalanges), the thinking function dominates the aspect of our character represented by the particular finger. A loop fingerprint enhances the social aspect of the thinking function. A whorl print represents originality and unconventional thinking. An arch print increases the practical quality of a person's thinking.

The shape of the fingertip also affects the quality of the thinking represented by the particular finger. A rounded tip is similar to a loop fingerprint. A spatulate tip is similar to a whorl print. A square tip is similar to an arch print. I'm generalizing. I'll get much more specific in the future when I write about specific character types. I'll also include case histories of family, friends, clients, and celebrities.

A majority of palmists look at the headline first to interpret how a person thinks. The direction and quality of a person's headline determines the direction and quality of their thinking. A headline can be short or long. It begins where the thumb meets the hand and may be connected or separated from the life line at its beginning. It can run straight across the hand, turn up towards the pinky finger, or dip deep into the heel of the hand. The quality of the line is crucial to its interpretation.

Dr. William Benham, the father of modern western palmistry, had an electric current theory. He believed that lines conducted a person's thought currents, just as electrical lines conduct electricity. If something impedes the current, it interferes with the function that the line represents at that particular time of a person's life. There are many possible obstacles on a head line: breaks, islands, dots, frays, crosses, stars, etc.

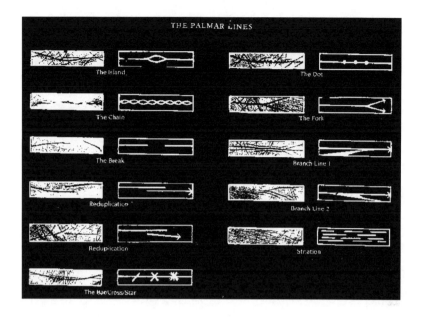

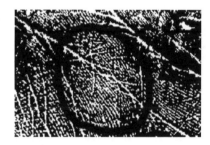

When I first began studying palmistry over thirty-five years ago, much of the writing on the subject was didactic and fatalistic. I had a huge island in the middle of my headline (illustration is not my hand) extending over a four or five-year period.

Older palmistry writings described a state of insanity, possible institutionalization, or at best, a state of utter confusion for that period. Needless to say, I was worried.

I called my brother, Gary, who was becoming a psychiatrist at the time. I explained my situation and expressed my fears. Gary asked me what the quality of the line was like after the island. I told him that it was strong and clear. He replied, "Don't worry about it. You'll figure out what it is when you get there, deal with it as you go through it, and understand it when it's over."

Gary was right. I did get there, go through it, and ultimately understand it. Knowing it would end made it a lot easier to tolerate. That's a huge advantage of being able to see your challenges in your hands.

Feeling Type

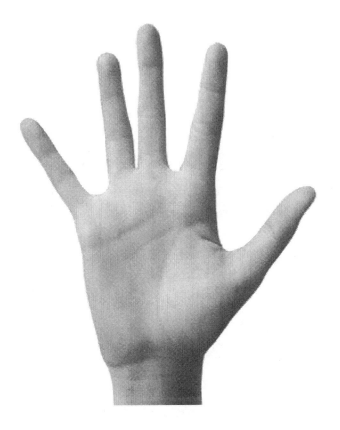

Feeling types have long rectangular palms and long fingers, which (unlike the photo) they normally hold closely together. As the most intuitive, empathic, and sensitive of all types, feeling types live deep in the world of their emotions. They're the hardest of the four basic archetypes to understand because they hide their true selves by avoiding emotional confrontation. Because they're very vulnerable, they need to feel protected and secure. Having structure, organization, and detail makes them feel more stable.

Feelings are an integral part of their decision-making process. They're cautious and must learn to trust others. Once trust is earned, their loyalties run deep. They get along best with other Feeling types and with Practical types who are the most responsible, reliable, and dependable of all types. It's not easy for Feeling types to trust Intuitive and Thinking types. They're afraid they'll be stuck dealing with the emotional fallout when idealism, enthusiasm, and interest wane (and they do.)

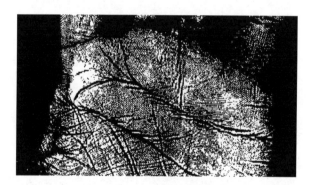

No matter which of the four basic types you are, everyone has a feeling function. Most palmists observe a person's emotional health in the qualities and directions of their heart line. A heart line begins under the pinky finger and extends across the hand toward the index finger. The line itself can have many qualities (heart line in illustration is chained.)

Heart lines may extend gracefully toward the index finger, curve up towards the middle finger, or dip down towards the head line (illustration shows all three.) If the line extends upward between the index and middle fingers, it symbolizes that the person is reticent to verbalize their feelings. It's much easier for the owner of this line to show affection or anger than talk about their emotions.

A long graceful heart line extending to the index finger is romantic and idealistic. People with these heart lines tend to see their potential partners and lovers more as they'd like them to be than how they really are. Talking about feelings is important to people with long heart lines. They're not 'hop in the sack' types, so a little candlelight and flowers go a long way to warming them up. As sentimental beings, they frequently cry during predictable old movies.

A person with a heart line that dips down to touch their head line needs to be in control of their feelings. These people compartmentalize, rationalize, and analyze their feelings instead of verbalizing them. No matter how good the physical chemistry is, the analyzer and the romantic don't make a particularly good long-term match as partners.

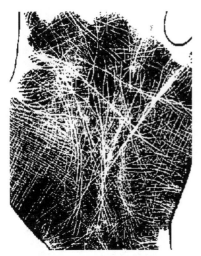

Many lines in the palm of a hand indicate a person with a lot of nervous energy. I usually suggest they stay away from caffeinated beverages. They wake up wired and easily tire from too much emotion. It takes little to make them overwrought.

They're extremely sensitive and naturally empathic, which makes them a magnet for strays and fixer-uppers. When you see a hand like this, don't begin by picking away at details. These people are sponges and very impressionable. They may hear the worst, even if you didn't say it. Whatever you tell them, they'll never forget it. Be constructive and helpful. I always find something to leave them feeling hopeful about.

Each of the four basic archetypes (Intuitive, Practical, Thinking, and Feeling) can be broken down into three specific character types by determining whether they're better at initiating, maintaining, or adapting. The Feeling type becomes the Nurturer, the Lover, and the Believer. I'll begin discussing specific character types in the future when I've finished generalizing about basic palmistry.

Three Modalities

INITIATORS have boundless energy and enthusiasm when they feel inspired and passionate. Powerful ambitions combine with magnetic personalities to compel them to take action and achieve their goals. Initiators are best at beginning projects and less inclined to maintain or complete them, especially when they get mundane or routine. These energetic personalities wield enthusiastic handshakes that are frequently enhanced by openly held fingers, low set thumbs, and resilient pink elastic skin. Their head and life lines are often separated where the thumb joins the hand.

Flash Rosenberg, an initiator, is a wonderful friend, Guggenheim award winning visual artist, photographer, performance artist, writer, and artist in residence for 'LIVE from the NY Public library'.

BUILDERS are great at maintaining what already exists. They say what they do and do what they say to the best of their abilities. You can depend on them to come up with a logical and practical solution for almost anything. Builders have firm honest handshakes. Their hands and fingers tend to have stiffer joints than the other two modalities. Large stiff thumbs represent abundant will, supported by dogged determination, and relentless persistence. Their greatest challenge is to embrace change and not procrastinate at beginnings and endings.

In general, round full balls of the thumb belong to givers and lovers of home, food, comfort, nature, children, and art. Square shaped fingertips and developed knots symbolize a practical, responsible, reliable, and dependable nature. More cautious types with fingers held closely together tend to be better team players. A Builder's head and life lines are often intertwined where the thumb joins the hand.

This is my dentist, Dr. Nathan Bryks. I knew I was in good hands the moment we met. He's as solid as the Rock of Gibraltar, a great craftsman, and a truly compassionate, competent, and caring person. With that large ball of the thumb he appreciates everyone and everything. He hums music while he mines my teeth for cavities. If I have to have someone digging around in my mouth, I'm glad it's Dr. Bryks.

ADAPTERS have a warm handshake that conveys honesty and sincerity (which may not necessarily be the whole truth). They're very clever, hate conflict, and work hard to avoid any confrontation by honing the fine art of tact and diplomacy. Adapters have the most flexible and elastic hands and fingers of all three modalities.

Adapters help Initiators initiate and Builders maintain. They do what Initiators and Builders don't do or don't want to do. They're extraordinary communicators. I love language and words. It's no surprise that I've chosen to be a spokesperson for one of the most esoteric and obscure subjects on the planet. I'm trying my best to shift the paradigm of palmistry as a gypsy fortune-telling scam by being a crystal clear communicator and a credible expert on the subject. My plan is to encourage people to begin examining their own and each other's hands and sharing valuable information about themselves and each other.

Twelve Types

Every hand has a dominant mythological archetype or combination of archetypes that correspond to the person's dominant astrological signs (which may or may not be their sun, moon, or rising sign). Whether you're looking through the lens of astrology or palmistry, when you multiply four elements by three modalities, you get twelve distinct types that comprise humanity's metaphysical family.

Each of the hands on the next page has a fascinating and compelling tale to tell that fits its archetype perfectly. I plan to share those stories in my next book. While describing each hand in intimate detail, I'll link the archetypes to the person's psychological patterns and behavior. Readers will come to understand how palmistry really works as they explore various hands and the narrative that goes with them.

TWELVE TYPES *INITIATORS* BUILDERS *ADAPTERS*

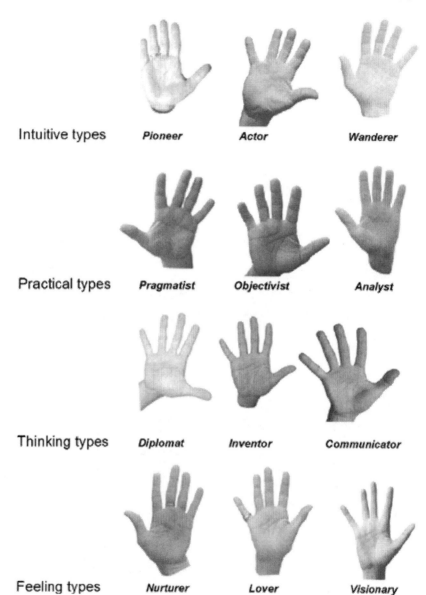

	INITIATORS	BUILDERS	*ADAPTERS*
Intuitive types	*Pioneer*	*Actor*	*Wanderer*
Practical types	*Pragmatist*	*Objectivist*	*Analyst*
Thinking types	*Diplomat*	*Inventor*	*Communicator*
Feeling types	*Nurturer*	*Lover*	*Visionary*

Learning to Judge Hands

No two hands are alike. Notice the difference between your own two hands. The hand you normally write with is your dominant or conscious hand. It reveals what you've done, are doing, and are likely to do with your talents and challenges. The other hand is your unconscious mind.

Once you identify four basic types, the real skill to reading hands is learning to judge hands. That takes practice and learning to use your natural intuition. It's vital to get the "big picture" first. When judging the qualities of hands, it helps to think of extremes. The texture of a person's skin can range from the velvety softness of a baby's butt to the calloused coarseness of coal miner's hands. You'll rarely see contrary qualities together in the same hands. People with opposite qualities seldom have much to do with one another. Debutantes don't dine with ditch diggers.

Whether a person's basic skin type is whitish, brownish, reddish, or yellowish, palms still contain varying colors. Rosy-pink is healthiest. It's frequently found in the ball of the thumb and beneath the index finger. Red color can mean too much energy, passion, anger, or rage. White is the opposite extreme and usually denotes a coolness or lack of energy and ardency. Hands and fingers can be extremely flexible, bending back at every joint. They can also be so stiff that you can't budge them with a nutcracker. Who do you think is more stubborn?

Healthy skin is elastic. It quickly bounces back when pulled and pushed. If the consistency and elasticity of skin stays indented after squeezing, that person needs more physical exercise to build resistance to life's knocks. A handshake can vary from cold damp mashed potatoes that reveal laziness and apathy, to a rough, hard, hot, and dry vice grip that asserts dominance.

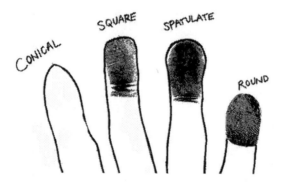

Classifying the thumb and observing the finger proportions and qualities in general is very important. Fingers can be long or short, smooth or knotty, and have tips that are pointed, conical, round, square, or spatulate in shape.

Are your individual fingertips shaped similarly or differently? Are your fingers straight or twisted? Are they spread widely or held closely together? How flexible are your fingers and each joint individually? Observe the proportions of individual phalanges (space between joints) in relationship to each other. Does one appear long or short or fat or thin in comparison to the others? Each finger has very specific meanings that are colored by hand type and by the individual qualities of fingers.

Gesture

Through body language all people are revealing who they are at each moment. Our bodies are in a constant state of change. Accurate interpretation requires a thorough understanding of the basic guidelines, a keen ability to observe, and lots of practice.

How do you hold your hands? Held openly, you have nothing to hide and are receptive to others. Held closely, you're cautious and may need to take more chances. People around you must work harder to build your trust.

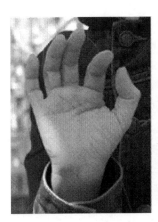 

A person's gestures may transform unconsciously during a consultation. I'll say, "Hold up your hands". My client holds up her hands with fingers held closely together and drooping forward. I'm getting a message that she's not feeling very good about herself. Maybe she's struggling with issues of self-esteem or spirituality. She's afraid I'm going to see something wrong or say something bad. I begin by discussing her most positive character traits.

Unconsciously and slowly her fingers begin unfolding and straightening out. In minutes her fingers are no longer drooping. She has nothing to hide. The new message is – Yes, I'm an open, loving, generous, person (for example).

Always speak to a person's issues from a constructive, helpful, and hopeful source. Positive affirmation goes a long way to facilitating positive change.

Fingers

Once you've established a basic character type, it's important to examine the fingers in detail to discover what kind of talents and careers a person is best suited for and how they manifest their potentials in the world. There are three phalanxes on each finger divided by two joints.

The first phalanx or tip of the finger symbolizes how we think and adapt our thinking to changing circumstances.

The middle phalanx represents our practical qualities and ability to take care of mundane tasks and responsibilities.

The third or bottom phalanx describes our material and physical needs.

Finger joints may be knotty (bulging) or smooth. Knots need order; no knots do not. Specifics will unfold as we examine each finger and character type.

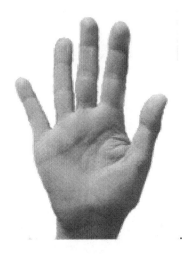

Dominant Index Finger

If your dominant hand's index finger appears long, (tip is more than halfway past the middle of the tip of the middle finger), projects forward, and has pink color beneath (all races), you're a planner, goal setter, and natural leader. As an ambitious professional, you're attracted to go-getters like yourself, steering far away from strays and fixer-uppers. Anyone looking for a free ride or unable to carry his or her weight will quickly lose your respect.

Many dominant index fingered people are of medium height with generously proportioned bodies. They frequently have wide chests, high foreheads, widely spaced kind eyes, and round faces with wavy hair.

These individuals enjoy being married and need a partner as much as they need a lover. Relationship challenges often result from obsessive or controlling behavioral patterns and judgmental, critical attitudes. False pride, gluttony, vanity, and bossiness are weaknesses that these individuals can overcome by practicing moderation and steadily earning their success.

Although, long index fingered folk are naturally healthy types, they must be careful not to overindulge in rich food and drink. As their physical sense is taste, temptation is strong. They love rich exotic foods, luxurious desserts, and fine wine. If they don't take good care of themselves, they're prone to blood disorders, liver trouble, diabetes, stroke, high blood pressure, and problems with hips, thighs, and throat.

Many popular journalists, judges, lawyers, politicians, producers, promoters, priests, speakers, salespeople and most of the finest and worst chefs have dominant index fingers.

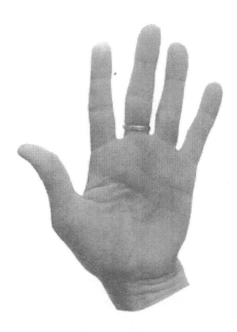

Dominant Middle Finger

The middle finger is considered the balance wheel of the hand. Notice how the strong middle finger in this photo appears to magnetically draw the other fingers toward it. Less inclined to marry than other types, this individual needs a lot of personal space. He's dependable, organized, efficient, patient, and a very loyal friend. A satirical sense of humor sometimes disguises his very serious nature. His greatest challenges result from obsessing on feelings of responsibility, obligation, and guilt. Being overly responsible and self-critical is a sure path to frustration, fear, and depression for individuals with dominant middle fingers.

Dominant middle-fingered people are frequently tall, slender, and angular in appearance. Pure types have dark hair, large bones, stern features, and bland complexions. Their prevailing physical sense is smell. Many love string instruments and prefer classical music with a tinge of sadness. They may eventually have problems with teeth, knees, ligaments, rheumatism, hardening of the arteries, hemorrhoids, varicose veins, and deafness in the left ear.

 If the middle finger leans toward the ring finger, you have an individual with a strong need for privacy. The moment he feels confined, controlled, or restricted, he gets cranky and irritable. Notice the crooked middle finger on Donald Rumsfeld's left hand. I'll bet he's cranky. Abe Lincoln and Clint Eastwood are quintessential dominant middle-fingered types.

Many conservative business people, technical individuals, craftsmen, writers, therapists, night watchmen, master criminals, morticians, undertakers, and derelicts have dominant middle fingers. Individuals with dominant first phalanges on the middle finger lead the way in research, science, mathematics, and humor.

Have a dominant middle-fingered boss? You'd better do your homework with a very sharp pencil. Precision and realism are required, don't be late and don't make excuses. Assume responsibility. If you're pragmatic, reliable, and dependable, you'll avoid criticism.

The middle finger is always the longest finger. Sometimes, however, it appears short relative to the index and ring fingers, which reveals a need for more structure, discipline, and focus. Harnessing these qualities is especially hard for these people. Healthy use of will power is essential.

The middle finger is the finger of fate. It's where illusion (or delusion) and reality meet. No matter what else is going on in your hands, the middle finger makes you face the facts and do whatever needs to be done. It always requires work on your part. There's a remedy for most maladies and the middle finger is the first place to look for solutions to challenges. If you don't do the work, it can show up in many ways in your hands.

A grill (which I call schmutz), for example, is a bunch of lines crisscrossing in every direction. Under the middle finger, this is a sure sign of frustration resulting from not doing what needs to be done. People with grills beneath their middle finger are their own worst critics. They need to lighten up, buckle down, and bite the proverbial bullet. Accomplishing one little step at a time is the best remedy for becoming frustrated and overwhelmed, which will gradually reduce and eventually erase the grill. A truly healthy person will have a strong healthy middle finger.

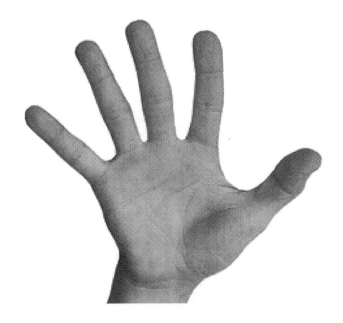

Dominant Ring Finger

While dominant index fingered folk are the most ambitious, and middle finger types are the most serious, ring-fingered people are the happiest. The ring finger is called the sun finger, symbolized by Apollo, who hauls the sun across the sky each day in his chariot. Authentic Apollo types are handsome, beautiful, brilliant, charming, graceful, artistic, and always successful on the inside. When the ring finger dominates your hand, you're versatile, adaptable, creative, and expressive.

Being so brilliant and having so many natural talents and abilities has its downside. It's easy to spread yourself too thin (the proverbial "jack of all trades"), or spend way too much time being concerned with outward appearances, or allow yourself to be tempted by casual attractions.

Abundant energy and natural charisma makes the sun type irresistible. They enjoy being married, however, they have very high expectations of their mates, which can lead to disappointment.

If you're an Apollo type, you're a generally healthy type, medium height, and naturally muscular and athletic. Your dominant sense is sight. Your physical weaknesses are eyesight, circulation, and heart problems.

Dominant ring fingered people are lucky. When they trust their gut and take calculated risks, they often succeed. I've read the hands of many gamblers with very long ring fingers. They're biggest challenge is in knowing when to stop, as optimism and idealism cloud reality.

Many successful actors, artists, musicians, designers, and sales people have dominant ring fingers.

People frequently ask, "Do you read your own hands?" or "What do you see when you look at your own hands?"

I plan to answer that question, but first I want to tell a story. When I began trying to figure myself out over thirty-five years ago, one of the first things I did was to look for reputable palmists to read my hands. I managed to locate three highly regarded and dedicated professionals. The eldest palmist (in her eighties), had been a protégé' of William Benham, the father of western palmistry. The other two were palmistry scholars and practitioners of Benham's teachings.

The hand above is mine. The first palmist I consulted with, who became my teacher, told me my "Venus" was dominant. That meant that my large ball of the thumb along with the very flexible first phalange of my thumb was the distinguishing feature in my hand.

The second palmist told me that I was a "Saturn" type. That meant my middle finger was dominant, as it was long and strong with a high centered apex beneath it.

The third palmist told me I was a "Mercury" type. That meant my pinky was dominant as it was long and straight, and stood independently from my hand. She was an astrologer as well as a palmist and knew I had a stellium (four planets, including my sun) in Gemini in my horoscope. I also have a thinking type hand, square palm and long fingers, which reinforced her interpretation.

All three palmists gave me good readings, however, they were each only partially correct because they chose a strong secondary type as my primary type.

 What I see when I look at my hands usually depends on when you ask me. I see a dominant long ring finger with a spatulate fingertip and a whorl fingerprint. Beneath the finger are a high centered apex (pictured) and a clear line of reputation. I envision tremendous potential for success, satisfaction, and fulfillment. I also see my challenges and obstacles.

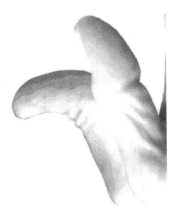

My first giant obstacle was learning to manage my strong "Venus". Along with my huge appreciation of art, music, nature, chocolate, and all things beautiful, came a complete lack of discipline, structure, and focus. I didn't know how to say "No". I also had an insatiable lust for sexual satisfaction.

I had to learn to embrace and strengthen my middle finger in order to harness my ball of the thumb. It wasn't fun and took almost twenty years of working at it to learn to exercise my will power in healthy ways.

I also had to stiffen the thumb on my conscious hand to a point where I could become more conservative with my ever-dwindling time and energies (the thumb on my unconscious hand is still very flexible at the first joint). My strong pinky made it easy to learn new things, but with that came immaturity and a resistance to growing up. It took me thirty-eight years to marry and forty-five years to become a parent, the two best decisions of my life.

I look at my hands and see an aging Apollo who still wants to shine brilliantly, a strong Mercury (pinky) who can help him communicate, a healthy Venus (ball of thumb) who still has a huge desire to give, and a slightly crooked Saturn (middle finger) who tells him that he needs to always stay humble and continue to remain structured, disciplined, and focused to earn his good luck.

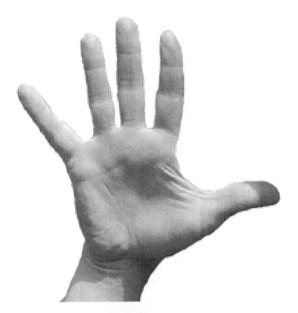

Dominant Pinky Finger

This powerful looking pinky finger belongs to a communicative, curious, and quick-witted individual. Dominant pinky fingered people are bottom liners. They're quick thinkers, excellent communicators, and aware that if their presentation doesn't add up, they won't make the sale.

Although they're childlike and cherish their freedom, they often end up marrying someone like their mother or father. They love children and will bear any burden for family. Dominant pinkies lead the way in science, law, medicine, writing, banking, and accounting.

Hermes is the Greek god attributed to the pinky finger. Peter Pan (adolescence), Puck, the Knight of Swords, the Court Jester, the Magician, Thoth, Loki, and Mercury are all manifestations of Hermes. These clever tricksters are all fabulous communicators and archetypes of wisdom.

Your own early family dynamic may be observed in the way your pinky is set on your hands. If it's very short or low set, trust is a major issue. Many women who have very low set pinkies have told me that they have trouble having orgasms. Their real challenge is in trusting themselves and others enough to have real intimacy. The pinky finger emphasizes technical, language, and family, in addition to sexual potentials.

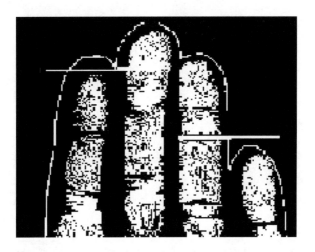

The pinky finger is normally the shortest finger. To determine whether the pinky is considered long or short, look to where it lines up with the ring finger. When the tip of the pinky finger is above the crease between the first and second phalange of the ring finger, it's considered long. When the pinky finger is shorter than that crease in the ring finger, it's considered short. Hermes was the shortest of the gods.

A dominant pinky fingered person tends to be short in stature. His or her body and face are slender, with expressive hands, dark hair, and penetrating eyes with crow's feet in the corners. Ed Harris is a great example. Pinky fingered folk are very youthful looking with men frequently having thin beards. Johnny Depp is a Mercurial type. Most Mercurial types are androgynous and many (although they may not know or admit it) are bi-sexual. David Bowie is a perfect illustration. Michael Jackson (Peter Pan) actually lived in his very own Neverland.

The pinky finger's dominant physical sense is hearing. Pinkie fingered people prefer small musical instruments that require a lot of dexterity. Their health issues center around the nervous and bronchial systems. They may have problems with headaches, thyroid glands, memory loss, and speech impediments. Healthy Mercurial types can be intuitive geniuses and great judges of character. Their liabilities are trickiness, fickleness, nervousness, restlessness, and superficiality. People preaching on soapboxes, most pickpockets, and a majority of con artists have dominant pinkies (most inwardly curving).

Mercurial types make great lawyers, doctors, orators, writers, engineers, teachers, accountants, bankers, shopkeepers, and magicians. I work at special events with many great magicians. These amazing tricksters are Mercurial with dominant pinky fingers. They surprise and astound by deceiving the eye and mind.

Is this man telling the truth?

The chirological equivalent of Pinocchio's nose is an inwardly curving pinky finger. If your pinky finger curves inwardly, you typically hate confrontation and spend way too much of your time behaving in ways that work. You've spent so much of your life acting and bending the truth that you aren't even aware you're doing it. Most curved pinky fingered people learned early in life that "nice" works. Their primary challenge is that "nice" ends up being safe instead of satisfying. Curved pinky fingered people are peacemakers. They try to fix other people. If you're one of these people, be yourself and not whoever you think everyone else wants and needs you to be.

Gold and diamond rings are often found on the pinky finger of acquisitive people. Pinky rings can symbolize the sublimation of sexual energies in order to accomplish something requiring a lot of energy.

I recently examined a group of fifty young men and women, all born into wealthy families in the 80's. Considering the prosperity of the period, it seemed a paradox to me that every single individual had an obviously short phalange on the bottom segment of the little finger of his or her dominant hand. The bottom phalange represents the material world. Money will never be the motivation for this particular group's career choices. Family issues and personal values will drive these individuals.

Fingers (Part 2)

Thick-fingered folk (especially the bottom / third phalange) have more desire for food and sensual pleasures. Thin-fingered people have more interest in nutrition and diet. I've seen very large people with narrow third phalanges. They've got a much easier time losing weight than their thick-fingered cousins because physical temptation is less strong. Jack Sprat will help you remember.

Jack Sprat ate no fat
his fingers were so lean
whenheldcloselytogether
floods of light passed in between
about sweets a care
Jack could not give
for Jack Sprat ate to live

Jack's wife had fingers obese
e v e n   s p r e   a   d
lightcouldnotpassthroughacrease
she could not resist any treat
for Jack's wife lived to eat

No matter what your fingers say about you, you still have to live your life. If the consistency of your hands is hard and your fingers stiff, you'll battle change with every last molecule in your body. "Letting go" will be a major life theme for you. Making `good sense' is essential to your well-being. If your hands are soft and fingers very flexible, you'll conjure every rationalization possible to procrastinate and not focus your energies. Needing "discipline, structure, and focus" will be your major life theme. Remain patient and create a framework that works for you. Learn to listen astutely.

Fingernails

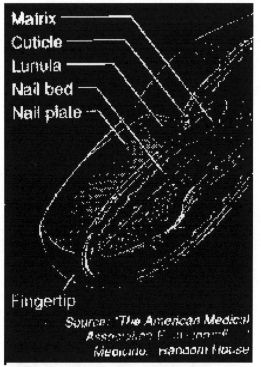

The nail plate emerges
from the matrix or growing
area to cover the nail bed.
Part of the martrix may
show as the moon or
lunula.

Fingernails are important. They come in numerous shapes
and qualities. Once you've determined the nature of the
whole hand and have examined each finger, its proportions,
knots, and shapes of tips, study the nails.

Any character can be open and frank with large broad nails or highly critical, argumentative, and nit-picky with very short nails. If you bite your nails, you tend to be self-critical or critical of others. If your nails are bitten down to the quick, you enjoy being contrary. You'll choose the opposite side of an argument just to make a point, even if you agree with the other person. If you know someone like that check his or her nails. Sometimes a person will bite only one nail. Apply critical qualities to the meaning of that particular finger. If you bite your pinky nail you may be critical about family, or anxious about your sexuality, or struggling with issues of communication, independence, control, or money. I began nibbling my pinky nails when I began editing this book.

Nails are windows to a person's health. What good are career or relationship potentials if a person doesn't have good health? I always ask female clients before coming for a two-hour consultation to remove nail polish so that I can observe the color and texture of their nails. Our nails protect the delicate nerve centers in the tips of our fingers. When nerve centers are operating in a healthy way, nails appear smooth textured, pink, and clear. When nerve centers are impaired, this leaves an impression on the nail texture and color and must be judged accordingly. A very fine and healthy person will tend to have fine and healthy nails, while a coarse person will have coarse or fluted (vertical ridges) nails. The more the nails appear to be fluted, the more nervous system challenges the person has. Fluting naturally occurs more with aging. Large moons tend more toward type **A** personalities. Small moons are normal. No moons often correspond to low blood pressure or a slower metabolism.

  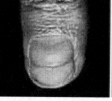 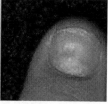

VERTICAL RIDGES   WHITE FLECKS   BEAUS'S LINES   IRON DEFICIENCY

Stress depletes calcium and zinc in the body, which shows up in the form of white flecks in the nails. Wherever you see flecks, you must apply both a time and stress factor to the meaning of that particular finger. A nail takes approximately six months to grow out. If you see white flecks in the middle of the nail on your middle finger, it may mean that three months ago you may have experienced a stressful situation in your career or work. If the white fleck is on the very tip of the index finger, then about six months ago, you may have experienced a blow to your self-esteem.

Misconceptions

Every so often a client will point out some tiny birthmark on the palm and tell me that another palmist told her that she was a high priestess, witch burned at the stake, prostitute, or washerwoman in a past life. I cannot confirm or deny such pronouncements. If a palmist sees past lives in your hands, it's not a product of the science of hand reading.

I sometimes have accurate and unexplainable insights while examining someone's hands. The best way to learn about past lives is to remember them. Many skilled hypnotherapists specialize in past life regression.

People frequently ask me to tell them about other people. It's impossible to obtain extended information about someone else from a hand. I use astrology and tarot cards for that. Sometimes a marriage, birth, or death of someone or something can be interpreted, but this is a nebulous area of palmistry and very difficult to pinpoint in time. The lines of a hand do function as time lines for a life.

Careful examination of lines and dermatoglyphics (finger prints and skin ridge patterns that seldom change) requires a quality set of handprints, a magnifying glass, and measuring device. Dermatoglyphics and timing are beyond the scope of this book. Richard Unger has devoted a large portion of his career as a hand analyst to finger prints. His book, LIFEPRINTS, is worth reading.

FINGERPRINTS

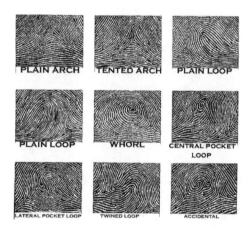

Keywords

Keywords embody concepts that unlock the doors to knowledge. They reduce an idea to a single word and are universal to all languages. In metaphysics, keywords are used to represent symbols and embody specific principles. When you learn palmistry, astrology, numerology, tarot, or any language for that matter, it's important to have a set of key words to guide you. Whether you're optimizing a search engine, exploring science, observing art, playing music, or examining human nature, the key to keywords is in their collective recognition and interpretation.

My metaphysical teachers always provided me with a list of key words at the beginning of my journey into a particular discipline. When I began studying astrology (over 35 years ago), I learned that our solar system and its relationship to the cosmos was the basis for constructing a horoscope. To an astrologer, planets are basic archetypes of nature and also keywords for specific energies, ideologies, and potentialities. As Apollo drives the chariot of the sun across the sky each day, he sheds light on all things. Sun is a patriarchal archetype that symbolizes consciousness and spirit. Moon is matriarchal and represents emotion and the unconscious. Mercury communicates. Venus senses. Mars energizes. Jupiter expands. Saturn contracts. Uranus revolutionizes. Neptune imagines. Pluto transforms. This is extremely superficial, but you get the point.

Planets are one of four basic elements required to interpret a natal horoscope. Astrological signs are adjectives that describe the basic qualities and energies of planets. Houses in a horoscope represent the areas of life in which planets and signs reside. Aspects are the relationships between planets, signs, and houses that challenge, enhance, and impel a person or circumstance.

Humanity consists of masses of harmonious and contradictory computations, permutations, and probabilities rotating and revolving through time and space. We're one big dysfunctional family, mainly because in our individual consciousness, all of time and space revolves around each of us.

It's impossible to define human nature with keywords, and yet keywords are necessary to understanding human nature. One challenge in relying on keywords in palmistry is that a majority of palmistry texts are obsolete cookbooks and notoriously confusing, full of stale ingredients and unreliable recipes passed down for generations. Inaccurate information and inadequate illustrations are cloaked in esoteric and technical jargon.

Palmistry keywords are not meant to define human nature, but instead, to evoke images, ideas, and feelings that give us insight into ourselves and others. That being said, I will attempt to generalize all of the literature of western palmistry using keywords. If you want to learn how to read hands, you can print out the list of keywords and consult it as you observe and examine hands.

Keywords in palmistry are derived from the basic formations and qualities of hands.

- Size, shape, and proportions of hands reveal a combination of four basic archetypes: Intuitive, Practical, Thinking, and Feeling.
- Hand texture, color, elasticity and consistency of skin, and flexibility of joints explain how we initiate, maintain, and adapt to new ideas and circumstances.

- Lengths and proportions of fingers, knots, shapes of fingertips, and qualities of nails represent how we relate and are fulfilling our potentials in our world around us.

- Fixed skin ridge patterns (dermatoglyphics), lines, and gestures reveal more detailed information about life path and circumstances.

Before proceeding, here are two very important ideas to keep in mind.

1. Always consider the dominant archetype. Remember that every detail is capable of modifying the whole and all other details at the same time. The basic shape and proportions of hands is the place to start. Finger lengths are crucial to understanding motivation. Shapes of fingertips flavor the thinking of the type. The development (or not) of knots modifies that flavor. No matter what else is happening, the color, consistency, elasticity, and flexibility of hands in general are critical to understanding a person's energy, natural resistance to life's knocks, and adaptability. Without a healthy thumb, it's hard to have a healthy life because will power or logic can be excessive or deficient. Reading hands is most satisfying when hand qualities are consistent, which they usually are.

2. There are relatively few pure types. Pure types tend to be extreme. They can be taxing to be around. Fortunately, most of us are mutts. Once you recognize a dominant archetype, look for a secondary type, which modifies the motivation and behavior of the pure type. With a dominant middle finger and secondary index finger, forget about middle finger melancholy. This person is a disciplined ambitious leader in their chosen career. If the index finger is dominant and middle finger secondary, a person's powerful ambition may be tempered or hindered by a lot of structure, discipline, and pragmatism. If the middle finger is dominant and the ring finger is secondary, forget about being a loner. This person is gregarious and much better at selling himself than the pure dominant middle fingered person. If the ring finger leans toward the middle finger, you could have a great craftsman or an overly responsible perfectionist. Your dialogue with the person will help you to understand how these qualities manifest in each individual. If a pinky finger is secondary, that increases shrewdness, adaptability, spontaneity, and a person's sixth sense. On the dark side, he could be the master criminal who can pick your pocket and rob your life savings at the same time.

Some people are harder to judge, as you will see as I begin to share stories of family, friends, clients, and celebrities.

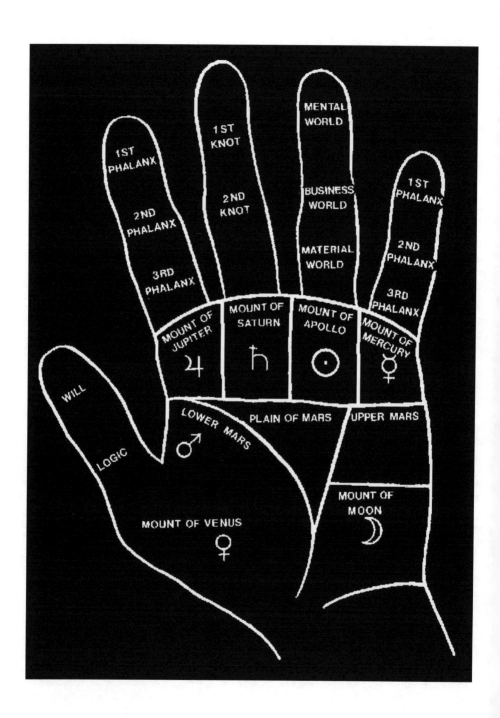

The following list is a modified version of a keyword list that was given to me by my palmistry teacher who tailored and shared the list passed on by her teacher. The purpose of keywords is to help students grasp basic palmistry. They're simplistic, intended to be an introduction to the subject, not concrete definitions of human nature. Keywords are meant to evoke images, ideas, and feelings that provide insight into self and others. As I've pointed out so many times, every detail should be examined and interpreted in the context of the whole person and all other details at the same time.

DOMINANT HAND: hand you write with, conscious mind, what you do with what you've got

PASSIVE HAND: subconscious mind, basic character, innate behavioral patterns, natural talents, abilities, and propensities

HAND SHAPES: relationship between fingers and palms

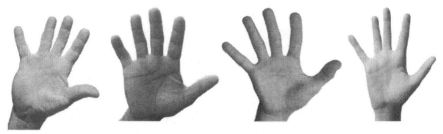

INTUITIVE	PRACTICAL	THINKING	FEELING
LONG PALM	SQUARE PALM	SQUARE PALM	LONG PALM
SHORT FINGERS	SHORT FINGERS	LONG FINGERS	LONG FINGERS

Long palm short fingers: Intuitive - large picture person, inspired, passionate, restless

Square palm short fingers: Practical - practical, responsible, reliable, dependable

Square palm long fingers: Thinking - social, communicative, versatile, needs space

Long palm long fingers: Feeling - most sensitive, vulnerable, protective, psychic

FINGER LENGTH: in relationship to palm / whole hand

Long: love of detail, suspicious, skeptical, sensitive, slow, thoughtful, careful, investigative

Short: intuitive, impatient, restless, easily bored, quick, hasty, needs to see the whole picture

FINGERS: positive traits based on dominant physical attributes

Index finger: ambitious, proud, career minded, goal oriented, natural leader, partner well

Middle finger: dependable, organized, efficient, patient, faithful, technical, strategic

Ring finger: versatile, adaptable, creative, expressive, likeable, dramatic

Pinkie finger: communicative, curious, quick-witted, clever, childlike

FINGERS: negative traits based on dominant physical attributes

Index finger: low self-esteem, critical, judgmental, controlling, indulgent with food

Middle finger: self-critical, frustrated, overly responsible, guilty, depressed

Ring finger: spread too thin, distracted, appearance oriented, gambler

Pinkie finger: restless, nervous, superficial, deceitful, con artist

SPACE BETWEEN FINGERS: relates to particular fingers affected

Wide space: need for freedom, sense of adventure, willingness to try new things

Moderate space: satisfaction with the status quo, not subject to extremes

Narrow space: cautious, private, takes direction well, doesn't rock the boat

FINGER TIPS: 5 primary shapes, can be any combination of fingers

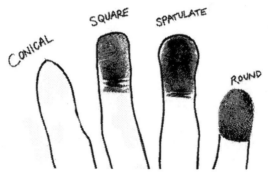

Spatulate: originality, inventive ability, unconventionality, needs activity, realism

Square: precise, orderly, practical, useful, punctual, systematic

Round: combines and balances spatulate and square qualities without extremes

Conic: idealistic, romantic, emotional, love of beauty & harmony

Pointed: dreamer, idealist, poetic, inspired, spontaneous, impractical, psychic

NAILS: takes six months to grow, timing = center of nail is 3 months, tip is 6 months

Long & broad: frank, honest, open, direct, balanced, healthy

Broad: physical strength, stamina, steadiness

Long & narrow: nervous, intuitive, lack of robustness, possible psychic ability

Small or short: curious, inquiring nature

Very short: (may be bitten) critical nature, nit-picky, argumentative

Cross ridges: trauma. Illness, health problems

Vertical ridges: nervous condition, easily stressed, increases naturally with age

Bulbous / whitish: bronchial / respiratory / circulatory problems, throat, lungs, and heart

KNOTS: located at joints of fingers, size of knot indicates degree of qualities

No knots: intuitive, impulsive, spontaneous, aesthetic, inclined to be social

Top knot: mental order, analytical, systematic, methodical, deliberate, thoughtful, careful

Bottom knot: material order, neat, organized, ordered, everything in its place, OCD

THUMB: how it's formed, size, and how it's set on the hands

Tip: will power, determination, ability to command

Second phalanx: logic, perception, judgment, reasoning ability

Large: (higher than middle of 3rd phalange of index finger) strong character, natural leader, guided by head, desires practical results

Small: (lower than middle of 3rd phalange of index finger) weak character, follower, guided by heart, sentimental, impressionable.

High set: cautious, private, less adaptable mind

Medium set: balanced, reasonable, sensible

Low set: (check position & how thumb is held) generous, independent, loves independence for others, impulsive, open adaptable mind, quick to grasp concepts

THUMB SHAPES AND QUALITIES:

Elementary: dense, heavy, coarse, tactless, no mental agility

Broad: determined, strong, physical energy & stamina, may be aggressive & blunt

Column: shapely thumb, strong will, tact, refinement

Paddle: broad tip with waisted 2nd phalanx, mental determination with tact & diplomacy

Nervous: flattened tip, lack of balanced energy, nervous mind & energy

Clubbed: (tip short & broad with short broad nail) often hereditary, obstinate, possible explosive reactions in difficult situations, crimes of passion, 'murderer's thumb'

Waisted: logic phalanx narrowing at center, refined logic, tact, mental agility, able to gently persuade, diplomacy

Stiff: practical, economical, stingy, willful, stubborn, cautious, reserved, traditional

Supple: (flexible – bends backward) extravagant, adaptable, emotional extremes, sentimental, generous, sympathetic, often have trouble saying 'no'

THREE WORLDS: hand as whole and individual phalanges of fingers

First world: mental & intellectual qualities, higher learning, ideas, thought, spiritual

Second world: practical, business, commercial, day-to-day routine & energy

Third world: baser, instinctual, animal nature, luxury, laziness, sensuality, material values, "what's in it for me"

BASIC LINES: beginnings, endings, meanings

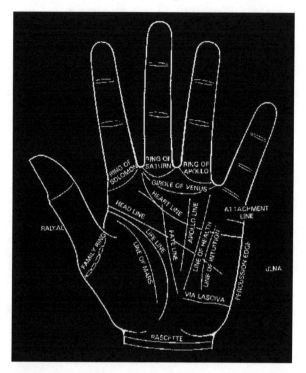

Life line: begins at thumb wraps around ball of thumb – about quality, not quantity of life

Heart line: begins under pinkie, traverses towards index finger, expression of feelings

Head line: begins near thumb, crosses toward percussion, how a person thinks

Fate line: begins near base of palm, rises toward fingers, quality and direction of career

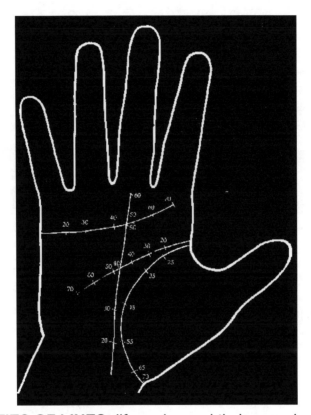

QUALITIES OF LINES: life cycles and timing can be roughly judged on lines

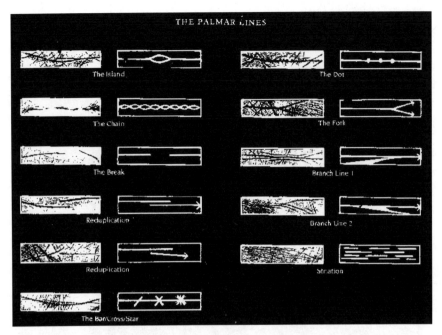

THE PALMAR LINES

Islands: obstacles, being divided for that period, indecision,

Chains: one obstacle after the other, chronic struggle about choices or directions

Dots: acute problems, possible headaches, heartaches, or physical obstructions

Bars: obstacle that can prevent the person from moving forward for a time

Breaks: usually an ending that implies new beginnings will follow

Crosses: challenges that need to be met, character building experiences

Forks: usually at end of line, taking two directions, conflict with decision-making

Grilles: frequently under middle finger, perfectionism, own worst critic, depression

Tassels: usually at end of line, energy dispersed or distracted near end of life.

TEXTURE: back of hand - think of extremes (baby's butt vs ditch digger) shows refinement

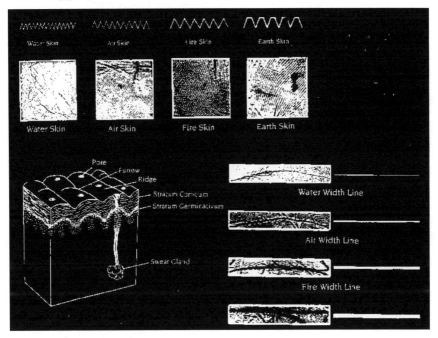

Fine: very refined, sensitive, cultivated (smooth with small pores)

Medium: normal, healthy, good resistance to life's knocks

Coarse: unrefined, earthy, may be vulgar (rough skin with large pores)

CONSISTENCY: shake hands, press under fingers, heel of hand, ball of thumb

Flabby: lazy, dreamer, procrastinator, desires ease and luxury, needs physical exercise

Soft: tends toward laziness, needs encouragement to develop energy

Elastic: considered healthiest, active, responsible, trustworthy, a doer

Hard: tends to be rigid, inadaptable, dense, best for physical labor

FLEXIBILITY: bend wrist and fingers back at joints

Very flexible: open minded, adaptable, versatile, distracted, extravagant, impressionable, tend to spread themselves too thin, possible mood swings

Straight: balanced, self-contained, in control, able to concentrate

Stiff: fingers don't bend, may curve inwards, cautious, narrow, stingy

COLOR: examine nails, palms, and lines

White: cold, distant, selfish

Pink: healthy, normal blood flow (especially ball of thumb and under index finger), warm, generous, sympathetic, appreciative

Red: intense, ardent, lots of vitality, physical strength, angry, violent, high blood pressure

Yellow: pessimistic, cranky, irritable, may drink too much carrot juice (changes meaning)

Blue: poor circulation, weak heart, may be seen at base of ball of thumb during a woman's menses, potentially serious health problem if seen at base of fingernails

Real Palmistry is the foundation for my next book Real Palmistry Stories. I'll be referring to it on a regular basis and linking hand facts to my stories so that readers can develop a deeper understanding of how palmistry works. Listed below are various ways of connecting to me.

Website: http://www.markseltman.com
Facebook: https://www.facebook.com/masterpalmist
Twitter: https://twitter.com/MarkSeltman
Linkedin: http://www.linkedin.com/pub/mark-seltman/3/119/602
Google +:
https://plus.google.com/104594853589957340176/posts
Pinterest: http://pinterest.com/markseltman/real-palmistry/
Youtube:
http://www.youtube.com/watch?v=LlxJP_lQMQQ&list=PLd503R
nLNmgiGHozJSzGxXGTi46D_pqWX

About the Author

 Over the last thirty-five years, Mark Seltman has read tens of thousands of hands of people of every age, gender, race, color, size, shape, career, and socio-economic diversity. He examines hands of celebrities, billionaires, corporate executives, and everyone who works for them. He's read Martha Stewart, Katie Couric, Star Jones, Kevin Kline, Kyra Sedgwick, Barbara Corcoran, Dave Brubeck, Maurice Sendak, and many other celebrities and their families. He's also observed hundreds of criminally insane people's hands at Kirby Forensic Psychiatric Center in NYC.

Mark has appeared on ABC The View, CBS Martha Stewart Living, CBS Evening News, FOX Good Day NY, Lifetime TV, Queens, and WNYC. He's been featured in the New York Times, New York Newsday, Daily News, Village Voice, New York Magazine, INSTYLE Magazine, Family Circle, Modern Bride, Manhattan User's Guide, and Astrogirl Magazine. Mark is featured in *100 Top Psychics and Astrologers in America 2014*.

Mark counsels individuals and couples, entertains at corporate events, and works for causes like: AIDS, Cancer, Cystic Fibrosis, Schizophrenia, Arts Education, and Healthy Environment. He taught Metaphysics 101 at the Cooper Union for the Advancement of Science and Art in NYC for five years, and has spoken or taught workshops and classes at the New York Open Center, The Learning Annex, Source of Life Center, Hunter College, Pace University, Fashion Institute, Marymount Manhattan College, and at the Theosophical Society in New York City.

32305908R00093

Made in the USA
Middletown, DE
30 May 2016